HOPI SUMMER

# HOPI SUMMER

## Letters from Ethel to Maud

Carolyn O'Bagy Davis

RIO NUEVO PUBLISHERS

TUCSON, ARIZONA

Rio Nuevo Publishers®
P.O. Box 5250, Tucson, Arizona 85703-0250
(520) 623-9558, www.rionuevo.com

Library of Congress Cataloging-in-Publication Data

Davis, Carolyn O'Bagy.
Hopi summer : letters from Ethel to Maud / Carolyn O'Bagy Davis ; foreword by Marlene
Sekaquaptewa.
     p. cm.
Includes bibliographical references.
ISBN 978-1-933855-08-0
1.  Muchvo, Ethel Salyah—Correspondence. 2.  Melville, Maud Seamen,
1880—Correspondence. 3.  Hopi women potters—Arizona—Correspondence. 4.
Hopi Indians—Correspondence. 5.  Women art collectors—Correspondence. 6.
Hopi Indians—Social conditions. 7.  Arizona—Social conditions.  I. Title.
E99.H7M843 2007
979.1'0520922—dc22
                          2007007686

Design: Karen Schober, Seattle, Washington.

Printed in United States of America.

10   9   8   7   6   5   4   3   2

*Dedicated to Emory Sekaquaptewa,*
*who has devoted decades of his life to studying and preserving*
*the language and culture of his people: the Hopi.*

# TABLE OF CONTENTS

Polacca Arizona
aug 24. 1931.

Hollow Mrs Melville.
I feel little better now
so I am going write to you and
tell you about the baby. she was
there before the things came.
she born on Sunday night, that
day was august 9. but poor
me Mrs Melville. I had a hard
time night. I never did have
harde time when I getting this
anather one, but this time did
I have hard time. so I am not
very storm yet. but I feel like
to write to day. because I did
not tell you about the baby
she is a girl and her name is
Vivina. and her father is very
happy with her. and I hope

# FOREWORD

THE STORY OF ETHEL AND MAUD during the years of their friendship through letters, from the early time of contacts with non-Hopi people, is an inspiring look at the lives of some very strong and remarkable people.

Reading the story brings images of a time of remoteness, solitude, and a seemingly harsh way of life for this Hopi woman and her husband. The loss of so many children would make one a good candidate for severe depression! This is also a remarkable record of a time in Hopi history when the outside world began to make an impact on a very isolated group of native people who had a longstanding way of life.

It is amazing that the Pahaana couple with young children would undertake such a journey into unknown areas of the country with virtually no facilities for comfort and sanitation.

The chance meeting of the two women from such diverse backgrounds to establish such a deep and compassionate connection is very remarkable. The basis for the relationship seems to be that the Hopi woman needed to reach out for solace and compassion to deal with so much loss, and to try to deal with the illness of her husband, while the Anglo woman was fulfilling a charitable desire and also trying to gain an understanding of a unique culture.

Information regarding the activities of Anglo religious groups on native lands and their efforts to take away the culture of the people is brought out in the story through the indications that Ethel was being pressured to accept the new religion. However, she seemed to have dealt with the pressure in a way where she could use some of what it offered and still remain true to her identity as a Hopi person.

This is a remarkable record of a time of great change for a group of people with a way of life that was already very ancient. Reading the story brings tears and also a sense of great pride as a member of Ethel's tribe. In spite of her tremendous challenges she did accomplish her most important responsibility—of having the one daughter to carry on her clan legacy as a Hopi woman.

MARLENE SEKAQUAPTEWA
VILLAGE OF BACAVI, THIRD MESA
HOPI NATION
MARCH 21, 2007

# INTRODUCTION

SEVENTY-FIVE YEARS AFTER HIS 1927 MOTORING TRIP around the United States, in which he and his family covered 18,000 miles, *The Journal of Antiques and Collectibles* in Sturbridge, Massachusetts, published thirteen of Carey Melville's Hopi photos in its August issue. In a serendipitous coincidence in that summer of 2002, I was visiting my daughter, who was living in Massachusetts. I chanced upon a copy of the *Journal* during a visit to Sturbridge Village. Having recently written a book on Hopi quilts and textiles, which included Hopi photos from a private collection, I was struck by the similarity of the photos in my book to the 1927 Melville photos, and was also surprised to see a collection of vintage Hopi photos in an Eastern publication many hundreds of miles from the Hopi Mesas.

In the course of researching *Hopi Quilting*, I met with the daughter of Florence Crannell Means, a writer of popular Christian children's novels in the 1930s and 1940s who had focused several of her books on the missionary efforts of the Baptists working on the Western Indian reservations. From her journals, it was apparent that Florence visited the Hopi villages at First Mesa, Arizona, during the same weeks that the Melville family stopped to camp at Polacca.

*"Driving up the road to First Mesa." This steep dirt track was mostly a wagon road. The Gap is just barely visible where the road curves up and a bit to the right.*

Several of the photos in the two collections are nearly identical, perhaps taken just seconds apart or from a slightly different position, as though the two photographers were standing shoulder to shoulder.

I was fascinated to see the Melville photos in the *Journal*. A brief caption mentioned that the Melvilles had been especially interested in the Hopi culture in their nine-month-long trip around the country. Mr. Carey Melville took dozens of photos of Hopi people and scenes of daily life, and Mrs. Maud Melville kept a journal, recording her impressions of their time spent at First Mesa. Additionally, the Melvilles established friendships with several members of the Hopi tribe, friendships which lasted for many years. In fact, the brief days that the Melvilles spent camped next to the Baptist church at First Mesa exerted a profound influence on Maud and Carey Melville that endured into the last years of their lives.

After they returned East, Mrs. Melville corresponded regularly with a Hopi woman for several years, as well as with several missionaries serving on the Hopi Reservation. She continued to collect Hopi pottery and other forms of Hopi art. She studied Hopi music, hosted a delegation of Hopi leaders when they traveled east, and, for many years, gave slide lectures on "Hopi Indians— the Modern Cliff Dwellers" and "Music of the Southwest Indians." She even organized a show of Southwestern Indian art—Hopi pottery and kachinas, Navajo rugs and silver—in an effort to give financial help to her Indian friends, as well as to increase New Englanders' knowledge and appreciation of their beautiful art.

It began to seem less of a coincidence that I chanced upon the Hopi photos, and more likely that I was meant to see the Melville pictures. I had made a short trip to the Hopi Mesas years earlier, and then found myself returning again and again. Like Maud Melville, I was deeply affected by the Hopi country, the people, and their history. Looking back on that summer, it seems as though I had been fated to find the Melville collection, which led to an opportunity to meet the Melvilles' grandson, Robert Arnold.

Early on, after seeing the wonderful Hopi photos taken by Carey Melville and reading Maud Melville's diary and some of the letters she had received, I assumed that I would write a book about their 1927 trip and how the Hopi Mesas had captivated the Melvilles. My early assumption was that this would be the story of how Hopi culture had influenced an affluent, educated Anglo couple (*Pahaanas,* to the Hopis) from New England—people coming from a community that could not have been more different from the people of the ancient Hopi culture living in the barren, windswept canyon country of the Southwest.

But, like many stories, this one took an unexpected turn within hours of a trip to Hopi to begin researching the photographs. Robert Arnold had shared a set of his grandfather's photos, and I had printed an extra set in preparation for a trip to the mesas in 2005. I hoped to identify villages and areas where the photos were taken. I never dreamed that I would eventually meet descendants of people in nearly every one of the photographs. But it soon became apparent that not only could these descendants identify villages and places in the photos, they also *knew* the people. And, like people everywhere, the Hopis I spoke with were fascinated to see historic images of their communities. They pointed out the homes in the village images and talked about the families that had lived there. They were also charmed to see examples of early life in the villages. Older men remembered hauling water from the springs, carrying bundles of wood up the steep mesa trails, riding donkeys, or driving sheep into the stone corrals where they would be protected through the night. Women from First Mesa helped identify the potters, and all the basket makers from Second Mesa knew the story of Nellie and the huge coiled basket that she made and sold for five hundred dollars. Each one reminded me that the basket was so large that the door had to be taken off the frame to get it out of the house.

People looked at the photos of the villages and commented on which buildings were gone, while others now had different uses. A building for drying peaches was now home to a family, and other homes were nearly in ruins. Even the mesa had changed through the years. One photograph of First Mesa shows the Gap, a natural saddle between the east and west ends of the mesa. Several people pointed out that a huge mass of rock at the Gap had fallen away over time, and to look at First Mesa today, it almost appears to be two distinct mesas.

But it was the reaction of people looking at now-deceased family members— mothers and grandmothers and fathers and aunts and uncles—that was the most moving. Cameras were a rarity in the 1920s; few people had them, and virtually no Hopis owned cameras at that time. Most Hopi people have very few photographs of their ancestors, but being a people of deep and extended family groups, they treasure images of their relatives. Nearly every Hopi home has a wall of family pictures, although most of the photos are contemporary. If there are any older photos, they were generally gifts from tourists or from some of the many scientists, anthropologists, ethnologists, or archaeologists who have come to Hopi country over the past century to study Hopi culture.

I soon learned to expect emotional reactions when I showed the Melville photos to people. Two sisters cried when I showed them a photograph of their grandmother and great-grandmother. Another man had tears in his eyes when

*"The Gap at First Mesa." Since this picture was taken, the geography has changed significantly. Contemporary Hopis who saw this photo commented that several of the large, house-sized boulders have fallen away, widening the opening significantly.*

he told me that he had never seen his mother as a young woman. In a photo I shared with him, his mother was holding his older brother; both have now been gone many years. Other photos showed a young woman on her wedding day, as well as an earlier photo of her as a teenager. The man she had taken in and raised as her own son tenderly held the photos and told me that she just represented love to him.

One morning I met a Hopi friend for breakfast at the restaurant on Second Mesa before we went out to visit a family. Soon the photos were being passed around the room, and people came to our table to see the pictures. Then they called other family members who drove straight to the restaurant to see the photos. Our eight o'clock breakfast stretched to four hours, and one Hopi man even paid for our meal. He wanted to thank me for sharing the pictures.

And, of course, I did share the photos. I had taken extra copies of the pictures with me to give to people, but I was soon taking orders for still more

*"Two in Tewa." Cloris (on the left) is dressed in ceremonial clothing because this was her wedding day. With her is Helen Chouyou, her mother-in-law (Ethel Muchvo's sister-in-law), who would have washed Cloris's hair for her wedding. Her hair is tied in the married women's hairstyle,* torikuyi.

copies. Families asked me to print six and eight copies so they could be shared with other family members. But the sharing went both ways, and in a manner that touched me deeply. From my earlier studies of Hopi quilting, I knew that the Hopis are a very private and reserved people. For generations they have been studied and written about, often without their permission. Quite often the material that was written was incorrect, or contained information that the Hopi people did not wish to be made public. I knew that I had to be very open and clear about my intent to write a book about this collection. I also knew that I would have to be sensitive in anything that I did write. But with almost no exceptions, everyone was eager to share stories, and they were pleased to have their family story included. They shared wonderful histories of their mothers and fathers and grandparents, and they invited me into their homes and shared more pictures. They took me out to see the washes and cornfields and sheep camps.

I was deeply touched and warmed by the sharing and friendship shown by the Hopis I spoke with. And as I talked with more people on that trip, and on the many visits afterward, I soon realized that this book would not be about the Pahaana family that visited the Hopi; rather, it would be a glimpse into the lives of the Hopi people at a time when few visitors went to the mesas. The photos captured images of daily life, and the letters and the stories shared by the many descendants shaped a story of the lives of a people living in a remote corner of the American Southwest. For today, even for the unchanging Hopis, there has been change. There has been travel and technology, roads and education, hospitals and HUD homes, and solar energy and broad outside influences. And while the Hopis have held steadfast to a culture and tradition that is largely deep and unchanging, still, there have been changes. Even for the Hopis, some things are gone forever.

This story offers a glimpse into a time that the elders tell us about: when Hopi farmers ran miles to their cornfields out on the plains below the mesas, and when women walked down the steep, rocky trails to the springs to fill their water jugs each morning. It was the decade before the imposition of the Indian Reorganization Act, when the government created tribal councils,

*"Wapya—traded when a baby at Corn Rock." No one at Hopi today seems to know anything about this man, but most agree that he looks like a Paiute Indian. In starvation years, a baby given to a Hopi family would likely have a better chance of surviving to adulthood. One Hopi man, when asked about this photograph, recalled that in his grandparent's generation there was a Navajo man, sort of an uncle, who had been traded into his family and raised as a Hopi.*

upsetting the traditional clan/religious village organization. It was before the stock-reduction program, when the government established grazing districts and forced Hopi men to reduce their sheep flocks by 20 to 40 percent in order to reduce the erosion of grazing land. It was before the 1943 decree when the Bureau of Indian Affairs redrew the boundaries of the Hopi Reservation, taking the lands used by the Hopis for nearly a millennium and reducing the size of the Hopi country to just one-fourth of its former area.

The title for this book, *Hopi Summer,* came from the obvious fact that the initial contact between the Melville family and the Hopis occurred during that summer of 1927, when the family camped at First Mesa and Maud Melville formed a lasting friendship with Ethel Muchvo, a Hopi potter. But in a larger sense, *Hopi Summer* also refers to a bygone time in Hopi history, the golden summer of the period before increasing government intrusion forever changed many aspects of Hopi life. Thus, a final season before the introduction of twentieth-century technology, before the realities of changing times brought on by federal edicts, before the years of the Second World War, and before increasing tourism and the inescapable winds of foreign—Pahaana—culture swept through the Hopi villages.

_◎))_

A few words about the photographs, the letters, and Maud's Indian collection: Carey Melville's Hopi photographs remained in the family collection for decades. Some of the images were used in the talks that Maud and Carey gave to various clubs after they returned from their sabbatical trip, but little more was done with them over the years. The three Melville children had little interest in the photographs and seldom spoke of their round-the-country trip. They obviously were not as captivated with the Hopi people as their mother had been. Maud's grandson, Robert Arnold, was the only family member who expressed an interest in the artifacts from the trip, especially the photographs. Maud offered her wonderful collection of Hopi pottery, kachinas, and other objects to Robert, but he felt that they were much too important, and that there were too many items, to be in a private collection.

*"Sheep at the head of First Mesa trail." Several trails led from Walpi down to Polacca. There were stone corrals on ledges just below the mesa. Sheep were driven partway up the mesa into these enclosures at night for protection from predators and from raiding Navajos.*

After much discussion with Robert and other family members, Maud decided to donate all of her Hopi arts to the school that Robert attended; they had shown him many kindnesses and given him help well beyond the assistance normally offered by a university. The institution that Maud chose for her donation was Wesleyan University in Middletown, Connecticut. In 1976, nearly half a century after the Melvilles' 1927 visit to the Hopi region, she donated 181 objects to the anthropology department. Included in that gift were some of the letters from Ethel Salyah Muchvo and the First Mesa missionaries.

Even though Wesleyan is nearly a continent away from the Hopi Mesas, the university recognized the importance of the Melville Collection and organized a team of researchers to document the materials. Seven years after the donation, *Hopis, Tewas, and the American Road* was published. The book is a catalog of the collection and contains essays on Hopis and Tewas (Pueblo people who emigrated to Hopiland in the late 1600s from the Rio Grande country of present-day New Mexico, settling the village of Hano on First Mesa). The book also documented the history of Hopi pottery and the complex role of trade in the evolution of Hopi Indian art.

Although most of the objects were given to Wesleyan, Robert Arnold retained the photographs, boxes of most of the letters written to Maud by missionaries, and letters from Hopi potters Ruth Takala and, particularly, Ethel Salyah Muchvo. Being a photographic archivist, Robert realized that the negatives had to be professionally cared for if they were to survive the years. And thanks to him, this treasury of images still exists. The photos had little

*"Walpi—Miss Bancroft with Hopi children." Grace Bancroft had been a kindergarten teacher in Worcester, Massachusetts (the Melvilles' hometown), before she went to Hopiland. Carey Melville's fingerprint can be seen on the top left of this photo.*

information, and captions within quotations in this book are the words written by one of the Melvilles. It is likely that some of the captions were added in later years by Maud when she was elderly, because many of them are incorrect in identifying people, locations, and dates.

Many of the photographs show the ravages of the years and also the primitive conditions of their processing. Carey Melville developed the images while on the road, camped under a tree or next to the First Mesa Church at Polacca, where blowing dirt and sand made his work in the field even more challenging. Now and then a trace of a thumbprint can be seen on a photo, giving the viewer a sense that Carey has just finished developing an image and handed it over for viewing.

Many of the negatives were painted with a lacquer to protect them from dirt and scuffing during the trip. Over the years, the paint has hardened and

*Marietta Poocha and her children sitting on a rock in front of the First Mesa Baptist Church. Marietta was a member of the church.*

worn, and in many of the photographs the vertical lines of the brush strokes can be seen. But in spite of those small distractions, Carey Melville's artistic eye is brilliantly apparent in the images. He captured the work of a potter laying a clay coil on a bowl, a Hopi shepherd guiding his flock of sheep home safely for the dark night, and the deep, secret shadows on the ancient stone houses of the Hopi villages. He allows us to view the joy of a young bride on her wedding day, and a mother's love and pride as she posed with a child for an image that would hold her in time for eternity. Carey Melville's photographs are infused with a sense of the vast spaces of the West and the enduring strength of the Hopi people. They are a treasure, a gift that stretches across cultures and through the years.

*Matilda and Lawrence Lomavaya with their children: baby Neida, Arlene, and Willis, 1935.*

# EXPLORING AMERICA

IN 1927, CAREY E. MELVILLE TOOK A SABBATICAL LEAVE from his work as a professor of mathematics at Clark University in Worcester, Massachusetts. Melville was forty-nine years old, and he, along with his wife, Maud, and their three children, planned an ambitious automobile trip that would make a roughly rectangular circuit around the United States. Friends were shocked that they would undertake such a rigorous and adventurous trip. At that time, roads were rough and poorly maintained. The Melvilles would have to camp out and cook meals over a fire. There were few amenities for travelers, and camping was seen as a way of travel undertaken only by people who had few means. Such a trip would surely be a challenge to the refined, Eastern couple.

People at that time did not go to the Wild West; they went to Europe or the modern cities of the East Coast. The Melvilles were educated and affluent. Sleeping on the ground and cooking over a fire was a radical departure from their life at home in Massachusetts. On their travels the Melvilles climbed the Washington Monument, hiked up the Hopi Mesas, and trekked down into the Grand Canyon. The trip would also be a physical challenge. Setting up the

*Maud Melville standing on an overlook in North Carolina. Perhaps she was looking
to the West, anticipating the coming adventures with her family as they began their grand
tour of the country.*

*A map the Melvilles used to mark their 1927 route.*

tent and unpacking the trailer each night was heavy work. Additionally, there were the many, many times recorded in Maud's journal when she and the children got out of the car to push it up a hill or through a sandbank or out of a flooded wash. For this family, the trip would be filled with new sights of Indian pueblos and hogans, rattlesnakes and bears, blue canyons and red sunsets.

Carey Melville had a deep interest in geology, and he wanted to see the dramatic landscapes of the West—the Grand Canyon, Yellowstone Park, Mount Rainier, and the Badlands. Maud Melville, just two years younger than her husband, was willing to go along on this adventure, and, as parents, she and Carey felt that a transcontinental trip would be educational for their children. They believed that any teaching that the children missed in school would be more than compensated for in the education they would get on the road, seeing the landscape of America and learning about people and history along the way.

*"Hubbub" and trailer. The water bag was slung outside of the car, and blowing wind and evaporation helped to cool the water.*

*Crossing a cattle gate in Tensleep, Wyoming.*

Carey Melville was born in 1878 in Maryland, the oldest of ten children. His family moved to Chicago when he was fourteen. He graduated from Northwestern University and did graduate work at Johns Hopkins University. Carey met Maud Seamen at Northwestern in 1900 when she was twenty. She was the daughter of a Methodist minister, who, during his career, had moved his family from parish to parish throughout Illinois. Maud studied philosophy at Northwestern and graduated in 1903. She married Carey Melville the next year, and the couple then moved to Worcester, Massachusetts, where Carey took a position as an honorary fellow in mathematics at Clark University.

Twenty-three years later when the Melvilles left on their American road trip, their children were Maud, age fifteen, Robert (Bob), age thirteen, and Martha, who was nine. The family planned their trip during the fall of 1926. Maud stitched sleeping bags for everyone, and equipment for camping and cooking out-of-doors was purchased and shipped to Carey's brother in North Carolina; since the family was leaving in the middle of winter, they realized that they could not camp out until they reached the warmer country to the south. Carey bought a new 1927 Model T Ford, fondly named "Hubbub" or just "Hub," with a special power drive and a small trailer for hauling the camping gear, spare car parts, camera equipment, and water containers.

The plan was to leave right after the Christmas break and drive down to North Carolina, where they would visit family and pick up their camping gear. They would be on the road for nine months, returning to Massachusetts in time for the children, and Carey, to start school in the fall. The family set off on January 29, 1927, on a "wonderful, sunny day."

It is difficult to imagine today the adventure of cross-country travel in the 1920s. Automobiles were still a bit of a novelty, especially in rural areas where people still depended on horse power. In her diary, Maud often tells of seeing horse-drawn wagons carrying people and freight, and in Texas she was especially impressed to see traditional Mexican supply wagons pulled by ten mules. Gas stations were scarce, and the Melvilles often stopped when they entered a town to inquire where they could buy gas. In Darien, Georgia, they "ran down to ½ pint of gasoline." In Mobile, Alabama, they were driving around searching for a gas station when a man, also driving a car and realizing their predicament, stopped and offered his help, and gave directions.

Roads were rough and generally unpaved in the West. Maud noted a twenty-mile stretch of paved road in west Texas that was "like heaven," and she mentions having a flat tire nearly every day. Sometimes there were days when there were several "tire punctures," and Carey spent many hours patching the tires. One morning in April, he put ten patches on them. In early June, in Albuquerque, New Mexico, not even halfway through their trip, the Melvilles bought all new tires for their car and trailer.

River crossings were often interesting—or treacherous. Many crossings were by ferry, sometimes they forded a creek, and in Florida they crossed an "old rattle trap bridge over Satilla River." In Louisiana they crossed on a pontoon bridge, and when they entered a nearby town the speed sign read: "Go slow the undertaker has been on vacation." A bridge in Texas was very "high and *rickety*." In Texas they also encountered a "terrible road over rocky ledges." Bridges in New Mexico were cement dips with measured poles at each side to mark the depth of the water. It was up to the driver to make the decision to drive on through the water—or not. West of Albuquerque on the way to Acoma Pueblo they came to an arroyo they could not get across. So, with very few provisions, just cheese and crackers, they were forced to spend the night. They built a fire with dry cactus and cedar, and watched the moon rise over the tall mesa. Maud wrote, "No one in the world knows where we are."

Many of the tourist or car camps were so dirty that the family drove on, and often had to "tent up." In Alpine, Texas, Maud noted that the camp looked "horrid and hot." Flies at Camp Grande in El Paso, Texas, made sleep

*Crossing the Llano River in Texas. Stones piled across the river give the driver a guide through the water.*

*Stuck in the sand on a primitive "highway" in Texas.*

nearly impossible. But the Melvilles met many friendly people during the trip. There were many offers from people to camp in their yards, and others stopped by their camps to talk (people from so far away were a rarity). Some brought food, or offered advice about roads and travel conditions, and sometimes led them in their cars to service stations or camping areas. The Melvilles often camped behind service stations. In El Paso a man came to their camp to talk one morning because he had heard that there were people in town with a Massachusetts car. R. H. Judhuis was "Boston born & ancestored," and he was pleased to visit with people from his home country; he had driven over two hundred miles from Carlsbad to see them.

Maud's journal recorded expenses (in Terlinga, Texas, they had to pay the exorbitant rate of thirty cents a gallon for gasoline) and mileage (she drove for the first time on the trip in Florida), temperatures, weather, birds and other animals, and road conditions. In Florida, young Maud found a five-inch centipede in the tent next to her bed; in Texas, the centipede was *in* her bed. Weather was always a factor; they dealt with howling winds and days of pouring rain—and the resulting muddy roads. There were nights when their water froze, and days when temperatures climbed well over 100 degrees. They drove through huge dust storms in Texas. In McAllen, Texas, they stopped to visit relatives, and when Maud and her son, Bob, went to the canal for water, a "big wind storm caught us & then rain came. C & Uncle F. [Fred] came to rescue us. It was surely scary. I was mud from head to foot."

The Melvilles saw amazing sights. In Georgia they visited an old plantation. The slave quarters in the back were overgrown with vines. They saw an

*A "tent-up" in Florida. Young Maud, Martha, and Robert wait for their breakfast while Maud cooks on the portable stove.*

*A water crossing in Florida. Bridges were few, and often rickety.*

alligator farm, cypress trees and orange groves, and sponge boats in Florida. They saw a chewing-gum tree and a salt mine and oil wells in Louisiana, and a quicksilver mine in west Texas. Maud especially enjoyed seeing the variety of flowers throughout the trip. As they crossed the prairie in Texas on Easter Sunday, she filled nearly a page of her journal listing the wildflowers along the road. She also loved seeing the bird-of-paradise trees "growing *wild.*" In New Mexico they saw yucca plants and encountered some cowboys herding a group of wild horses. After sharing their water, they were invited to go to the corrals and watch the branding. At Hueco Tanks they saw Indian pictures (petroglyphs) on walls of rocks. Near Ramah they saw prehistoric cliff dwellings.

In Georgia they bought pecans for thirty-five cents a pound; in Florida they had grapefruit for breakfast (oranges were ten cents per dozen) and leather lemon pie; in Louisiana they had "native wild black berries for breakfast." On the beach they dug for coquinas, a type of small clam, and made coquina broth for dinner. In one camp they ate cabbage palmetto (the buds of which are known as "heart of palm") cooked with bacon; they tried boiled crawfish in Louisiana. In Texas they ate hot tamales, relish made of cactus, and *cabrita* (young goat); and in New Mexico they snacked on piñon nuts purchased for forty cents a pound.

Not only did the Melvilles see new sights and animals and taste exotic foods; as the family went farther west, the landscape became more foreign and dramatic. The Chisos Mountains in what is now Big Bend National Park especially enchanted Maud. She wrote that the mountains had "rare colors" and that they looked to her like "fairy" mountains. The temperatures climbed as

*A supply train in Texas. Each wagon is pulled by a team of ten mules.*

*On June 21, 1927, Maud noted in her diary, "All we can see is two-wheel tracks meandering across the desert toward the mesa." In the distance were the stark Hopi buttes rising up from the floor of the desert. On seeing this photograph, one Hopi man remarked that it was near Hand Pump Wash.*

they drove west through the desert country. On the nineteenth of May, Maud wrote, "Hottest breeze I ever felt. 106 in the shade." A few days later she made the droll observation that out West it was so dry, "things petrify instead of putrefy." But they were also seeing a land of strange and beautiful scenery. Carlsbad Caverns was so overwhelming that she could not even begin to describe in her journal what she had seen.

After several months on the road, the Melvilles became more accustomed to the wild and lonely country of the West. One night in June they camped near an ice cave in western New Mexico. It was such a beautiful night that Maud wrote that she "hated to go to bed. Last things I saw before I went to sleep were the glowing embers, tall pines & full moon floating in fleecy white clouds reflected in a thousand drops of water on the pine needles." At El Morro they slept under the stars and the light of the full moon.

It is hard to know what the three children thought of the trip. In her journals Maud usually just refers to them as the "3," as her entry on May 21 shows when they had a very late day and didn't make camp until after midnight: "3 *all* good sports, counted rabbits—75." The children were crowded into the back seat of a small automobile. Without air conditioning the open windows of the car let in hot, dusty air. (When it rained Carey had to stop the car and snap on the window curtains.) Of course, they sometimes quarreled and became cross. On March 25, Maud wrote, "on way out of camp had to stop & spank Martha." In Texas the family met A. J. Tippit, who owned the Mitre Peak Ranch near Alpine. His son Ralph brought his racehorse, Pancho, over to the camp for the children to ride, and young Maud "galloped over the prairie" for hours. It must have been a great change from the hours and days of sitting in the back of the Model T. And again at White Sands, New Mexico, the "3" ran barefoot over the pure white sand dunes composed of gypsum crystals. Maud thought them "vast mountains of sugar."

The Melvilles were a very genial family, but their trip did crowd them together for great stretches of time. It also meant that Maud and Carey had almost no time alone. One tender entry in her journal noted that she "watched moon come up with C. after 3 in bed."

## THE HOPI MESAS

*Never in my life have I been in such a place.*
*The thrills we have every hour can't be put in a letter.*

FROM MAUD MELVILLE'S LETTER HOME,
JUNE 24, 1927

ONE OF THE IMPORTANT DESTINATIONS OF THE TRIP was the
Grand Canyon in Arizona. But a detour to the Hopi Indian Reservation was planned because Dorothy Humes, the aunt of young
Maud's best friend in Worcester, was living there, serving as a missionary at the First Mesa Baptist Mission. The Melvilles had enjoyed
their brief visits to the Rio Grande Indian pueblos in New Mexico
and planned an equally brief trip to the Hopi Mesas. Their visit
stretched to eight days—eight days that profoundly and permanently changed the Melvilles, especially Maud, who formed a lasting
friendship with a Hopi woman, a pottery maker from First Mesa.

The Hopis are an old and mystical people. Their land in northeastern Arizona is bleak and barren, and while they are wealthy

beyond measure in tradition and culture, they are a people with few material goods, existing at that time through subsistence farming and the production of Hopi art for the tourist trade. And yet, for many people, the Hopi country has an irresistible attraction. After just one visit, people are compelled to return again and again throughout their lives.

The Hopis have lived in the Four Corners area of the Southwest for more than 2,000 years. Their ancestors are thought to be the people who built the cliff dwellings at Mesa Verde in southwestern Colorado, and Betatakin and Keet Seel in northern Arizona. According to their origin legends, the Hopi came up to this world, the Fourth World, from the Underworld, the Third World, at a place near the juncture of the Colorado and Little Colorado Rivers. Those people wandered through the Southwest, and they evolved into the Hopi clans that exist today. Eventually, over a period of many years, these clan groups arrived at what is now known as the Hopi Tutskwa, Hopi lands.

*The beautiful and dramatic village of Walpi sits at the northern end of First Mesa. According to tree-ring dates, the village was built about 1700. Hopi oral history relates that Walpi is where the first Hopi Snake Ceremony occurred.*

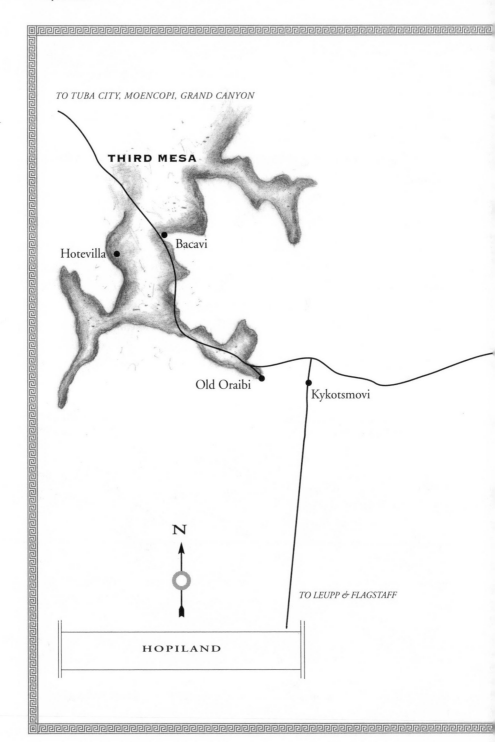

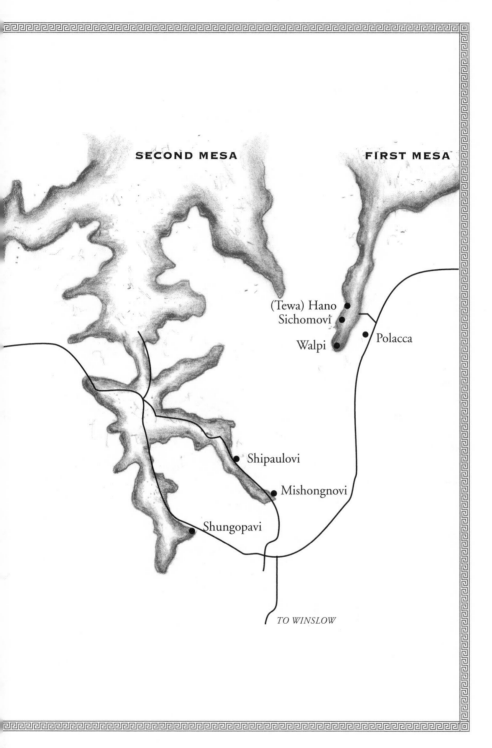

SECOND MESA

FIRST MESA

(Tewa) Hano
Sichomovi
Walpi
Polacca

Shipaulovi

Mishongnovi

Shungopavi

*TO WINSLOW*

These lands are located in northeastern Arizona on the three fingers of Black Mesa, known as First, Second, and Third Mesas, and their stone houses in the traditional pueblo villages are many hundreds of years old. There are eleven villages on the three mesas and two newer settlements, Moencopi and Tuba City, about forty miles to the northwest.

Hopi country is harsh and arid, with an average annual rainfall of only eight to ten inches. The minimal rain makes existence difficult, but the Hopis are excellent dry farmers. The people depend on supernatural help to survive, to bring the rains that nourish their corn and melons, to ensure good health,

*"View—top of Second Mesa." Mischongnovi is the old village along the skyline. There was an earlier village nearby, from the thirteenth century, but the people moved to the present location in the 1700s.*

*Melvilles and friends walking through Walpi. In a 1929 letter to Maud, Miss Ryan wrote that in Sichomovi, the middle village on First Mesa, a Hopi woman had died when she fell from the edge of the mesa. Today there are fences and low walls along the mesa's edge.*

to guide their lives. Hopi religion is complex and largely incomprehensible to outsiders, yet it is also mysterious and compelling to the many people who visit the mesas. To the Hopi people, their religion guides their lives and encompasses every thought and action. The demarcation between natural and supernatural, the "real world" and a world of myth, mystery, and ancient lore, is often blurred. There are spirits in inanimate objects and forces—the winds, the rains, the mountains, springs, and plants. Living beings—animals, birds, bugs, and butterflies—also possess spirits.

The Hopis are a profoundly religious people. Their beliefs and their ceremonies are complex and all-encompassing. Their daily lives are deeply entwined

with their religion and the ceremonies and rituals that are carried on throughout the year. Many of these rituals are performed in the kivas (underground
religious chambers that are closed to outsiders), but parts of those ceremonies,
commonly known as kachina dances, which are held in the village plazas, are
sometimes open to visitors. Kachinas are sacred beings, the spirits the Hopis
pray to (*katsina* is the correct form, and the plural is *katsinam*; however,
kachina is the most commonly used spelling to identify these sacred beings as
well as the carved figures, or "dolls," that are given to children by the kachinas,
and also are highly prized objects of Hopi art). At certain times the kachinas
come to the villages, and through the ceremonial dances and the priests who
participate in the sacred observances, the prayers of the people are carried to
the holy spirits. Tourists who are privileged to view these rituals come away
awed and deeply aware of the spiritual power of the dance, and of the Hopi
people. Even though the Melvilles did not view any of the ancient Hopi
kachina dances during their 1927 visit to the Hopi Mesas, they still came away
from their visit changed and forever enchanted with the Hopi people.

◎))

On June 20, the family left Winslow, Arizona, and traveled west to Two Guns,
where they met Chief Joe Secakuku, a Hopi who ran a curio store there. He let
the Melvilles leave their trailer at the store while they went to see Meteor
Crater. When they got back to Two Guns, Maud tried to pay Secakuku for
watching the trailer, but he refused to take any money. When she tried to buy
some curios, he told her to wait until she got up to the reservation where she
could find better and cheaper souvenirs. They traveled on and got gas at
Canyon Diablo. From there they turned north, but when they searched for a
spring, they found no water, so that night they made a dry camp by the side of
the road. There was nothing but desert all around them. In the dark they saw
the faint glow of light from a Navajo hogan in the distance.

In the morning they were up early. The sky was cloudless, and it was already
106 degrees. Maud wrote in her journal: "All we can see is two wheel tracks
meandering across the desert toward the mesa." The buzz of a fly and the bray of

a burro were the only sounds they heard in that still landscape. In the distance they saw an Indian on a horse, driving a herd of cattle. He gave a friendly wave.

On June 21 the Melvilles arrived at Oraibi on Third Mesa, where they stopped and bought gas (at thirty cents per gallon) and groceries; they also camped there for the night. They met and chatted with the trader Lorenzo Hubbell (presumably Hubbell the younger, John Lorenzo Hubbell's son). The Hubbells had trading posts in both Oraibi and Kykotsmovi, the village below the mesa, and the Melvilles asked Hubbell about the roads. Even though it was 112 degrees in the sun, something about Hubbell gave Maud "the shivers." The next morning they went east to First Mesa. On the way they passed a Hopi cornfield. A dry, dead sheep, propped up, with a rag in its mouth, served as a scarecrow. When they got to Polacca, the village at the base of First Mesa, the

*The Melville camp at Polacca, between the large Baptist church and the stone building that housed the laundry. The "wee dog" in the foreground is Piki, the stray that adopted Martha and followed the family all over First Mesa.*

first person they met was Ruth Takala, a Hopi potter. She rode with them, giving directions to the First Mesa Baptist Church, where they met the missionaries, Miss Ethel Ryan and Miss Dorothy Humes (like Miss Humes, Ethel Ryan was from New England; she was from Millbury, Massachusetts, a small town just five miles south of Worcester). The Melvilles set up their tent between the church and the laundry building. As they worked, several Hopis came to watch them. They were especially curious about their stove and air beds.

The next morning the Melvilles went to Mr. Womack's garage, just a short walk from the church. Womack had some baskets for sale, and Maud bought several. Then they drove up to the top of First Mesa, where they toured the three villages, Hano (Tewa), Sichomovi, and Walpi. Maud commented on the adobe and stone houses, and the old iron beds used as fences. They visited with many Hopi families and bought pottery from Lucy Lalo's mother in Hano. The Tewa people of Hano village are not Hopis but are related Pueblo people. They came from the Rio Grande country in New Mexico in the late seventeenth century. Their language is distinct from Hopi, but after two centuries of intermarriage they are often known as "Hopi-Tewas."

The middle village on First Mesa is Sichomovi, and Walpi is the ancient village at the far western end of the mesa. In Walpi the Melvilles climbed up to the third floor of the multi-storied pueblo houses and saw an old man who was watching a baby. He sat on the floor holding the child and sang an Indian song, accompanied by the shaking of a gourd rattle. To the Melvilles the sounds were like nothing they had ever heard before.

From Walpi they walked around the edges of the mesa and saw kivas and a sacred rock formation. They also saw eagles tethered to rooftops, as well as the eagles' burying place. Eagles play a vital role in Hopi religious rites and ceremonies. Each spring Hopi men with certain ceremonial responsibilities travel to the deep canyons and jagged cliffs that surround the mesa country in search of nesting eagles. The Hopi have used these sites for countless generations, and there are certain areas that are considered to be for the exclusive use of a particular clan (although today that country may technically be within the boundaries of the Navajo Reservation).

*Martha Melville standing halfway up the steps leading to the second-floor room of a Shungopavi home. An eagle is tethered on the rooftop just above her.*

As the men go to these clan places, they watch for an eagle soaring high above. Sometimes this search will take several days. After an eagle has been located, they will watch to see where it flies, in an effort to locate the nest. For ceremonial purposes, a young eagle is necessary, and it is best if the eagle is captured before it begins to fly.

The eagle is treated like a newborn child. It is carried on a specially made cradleboard and taken back to the village where its head is ceremonially washed and sprinkled with cornmeal, and it is given a clan name. The eagle is then tethered to a special place on a rooftop. While the eagle is in the village, young men hunt for small game to feed the bird, and it is treated as a special member of the family. In early summer, eagles and hawks are often seen on the rooftops in Hopi villages. One Hopi explained that the eagles observe the people through their daily work for the time they are in the village, and their presence serves as a reminder to people to observe proper Hopi behavior. And later, when the spirits of the eagles travel to the sacred home of the kachinas, they share all that they have seen in the villages. These good reports result in blessings upon the Hopi people.

In July the Niman ceremony (Nimantikive, the Home Dance) is held; this is the time when the kachinas return to their spiritual homes, one of which lies in the San Francisco Peaks near Flagstaff, Arizona. It is also a time when new brides in each village are honored. This ceremony lasts for sixteen days, and through the time when the kachinas are dancing, gifts are given to the children, as well as to the eagles. A male eagle may be given a bow and arrow and a female will receive a special kachina doll. The cry of the eagle heard in a village is considered to be a blessing to the ceremonial proceedings.

On the day after Nimantikive, the eagles are blessed and then smothered in sacred cornmeal. The feathers are taken, and the remains of the eagles are reverently buried in a special place outside of the village, at the eagles' burying ground. In her journal of 1927, Maud wrote about visiting that sacred spot. Today it would be unheard of for a casual visitor to be shown such a sacred site. It is likely that Maud was taken to the place by the missionaries, because the missionaries would not have respected the values of the Hopi religion. They were there, after all, to promote Christianity.

The feathers of the eagles are used in ceremonies, for making *paahos,* or prayer sticks, and the small downy feathers are tied to cotton string, *nakwak-wusi.* These downy feathers represent the breath of life. They are tied onto the corner of a bride's wedding garment, where the feathers represent the wish for a child to be born to the newly married couple. Other prayer feathers are tied to willow sticks and placed inside a house, on the ceiling in the wooden beams and rafters. These represent prayers for the health and well-being of the occupants of the house.

⟨◎⟩

The Melvilles visited with a blind Indian woman named Kunaa, who was grinding corn. They also watched a woman who was making *piiki,* and they all tasted some of these rolls of paper-thin corn batter cooked on an oiled stone

*Members of the First Mesa Baptist Church at Polacca. The woman standing in front of the door in the white dress is missionary Ethel Ryan. Ruth Takala's father, Hongavi, is seated to the left front.*

over an open fire. They thought it was "*very* good." Martha petted a little stray dog, and for the rest of their stay at Hopi, the dog, fondly named "Piki," for the distinctive Hopi corn bread, followed her everywhere. In the evening they went to a prayer meeting at the church. About eight Hopis attended, and the service was led in Hopi by an Indian woman named Sellie. Maud thought her preaching was "most impressive, *earnest*." Later Sellie brought some of her unfired pottery to show to the Melvilles. Maud chose several pieces.

The next morning some women came by the Melville camp to show their pottery. Maud was enchanted with the beautifully painted pottery vessels, and bought several. Later the family met Forrest Robinson, the pastor at Keams Canyon, along with his wife and son, William, who was Bob's age. Abigail Johnson, the missionary from Sunlight Mission at Second Mesa, joined them, along with three Hopi girls (Margaret, Elisabeth, and a third girl whose name

*When the Melvilles visited Nellie Quamalla at Coyote Springs, they found her working on her famous basket.*

was not recorded in Maud's journal). The group went south to Pliny Adams's ranch and had a picnic (Adams was a Hopi who was also a Christian convert). From there they went to Ispa (Coyote Springs), a spring located several miles south of Shungopavi below Second Mesa. At Ispa there were several buildings, simple houses used during the summers when the men were herding sheep and working in the fields. There they visited with Nellie Quamalla, a Second Mesa woman who was working on a huge coiled basket.

_⊙⟩⟩_

The story of Nellie's magnificent basket has become a legend among the Hopis. Nellie and her husband, Archie Quamalla, lived in the village of

Shungopavi on Second Mesa. Among the Hopis it is customary for a man to move to his wife's home at marriage, but that was not the case with Nellie and Archie. Nellie was from Shipaulovi (also on Second Mesa), but she chose to move to her husband's community of Shungopavi. Nellie had a sister, Violet, who also moved to Shungopavi when she married, so the two sisters lived near each other. In the summer, when it was time to shear sheep and also to plant and harvest crops, Nellie and Archie went a few miles south of their mesa home to Coyote Springs. At the springs there were five houses where they stayed with several other families. There was a hand pump at the spring to supply water to the families. Nellie's house had three rooms, and she had planted a small garden in the yard. She also picked the wild asparagus that grew near the pump.

*Tom Pavatea, Nellie and Archie Quamalla. Nellie posed with her magnificent coiled basket on the loading dock of Tom Pavatea's trading post at Polacca.*

Nellie and Archie had no children of their own, but they always welcomed visits from neighbors' children and from their many nieces and nephews. They were known as good storytellers, and one neighbor recalled that many of their stories were very funny and entertaining. At Coyote Springs, the Quamallas' nearest neighbors were Lloyd and Lydia Mansfield, from Shungopavi. Lydia recalled one special summer night when Archie and Nellie called to them to come outside. Nellie had tied a flour sack around her shoulders, and Archie had one around his waist, like a kilt worn by the kachinas. Then they proceeded to sing and perform a Long Hair Dance. Lydia remembered it as a night of great fun, as they all laughed together. It always stood out as one of the best evenings for her.

Lydia also recalled that Nellie was always making baskets. And the story of her biggest basket is still told on Second Mesa. In the 1920s, few Hopis had jobs; they subsisted on the crops they grew and the animals they raised. There was a small tourist market for Hopi arts; men carved kachina dolls to sell, while First Mesa women were known for their beautiful pottery, and the Second Mesa women made intricate coiled plaques and baskets. In that time, there were few tourists making the long trip to Hopiland, but there were trading posts in the area. Lorenzo Hubbell had stores at Third Mesa and at Keams Canyon, east of First Mesa. The nearest store was Tom Pavatea's store in Polacca at the base of First Mesa. Still, it was a long distance (about twenty miles, round-trip) for the people of Second Mesa to travel, often on foot, to purchase or trade for necessities such as salt or sugar.

Nellie knew of the difficulty in obtaining supplies, as she was often faced with the long walk to First Mesa. She had virtually no money, but she did have her skills as a basket maker to call upon. The story goes that she decided that she would make the largest coiled basket ever created by a Hopi, to raise money to open a small store on Second Mesa, where the neighbors in her village could purchase a few necessities. And by the summer of 1927 (the year that Carey and Maud visited the mesas), at the house at Coyote Springs, she had begun work on the famous basket. Most Hopi basket makers hold their baskets on their laps as they weave the coils around and around. Nellie's basket was 135 inches in circumference. She had to sit on a chair as she added coil after coil, and before it was finished she had to stand, walking around the basket as she added each row. The finished basket was nearly four feet tall (sixty-four coils from the base to the top) and just over three and a half feet across. Nellie wove three bands of geometric designs at the bottom of the basket, and then she wove in eight kachinas, including three Crow Mother Kachinas, finishing with a last geometric band near the top.

When the Melvilles visited Coyote Springs, they found Nellie working on the basket. Children ran in and out of the open door, and Maud wrote that "while Nellie wove on the basket, chickens [were] wandering in and out in the kitchen, corn hanging on the walls, the Hopi woman weaving without pause—a very impressive picture." The basket took Nellie at least two years to complete, and when it was finished, the door had to be taken off its hinges to get the basket out of the Coyote Springs house. Archie and Nellie loaded the huge basket into a wagon and took it to Tom Pavatea's trading post at Polacca, where it was said that he paid $500 for the basket, an enormous sum at that time. (This was at a time when pottery was selling for just a few dollars. Small pieces went for under a dollar, and even the famous potter Nampeyo was paid only five dollars for a twelve-inch bowl.) With that money, Nellie and Archie bought supplies for a small store that they opened in their home at Shungopavi. Buyers came to their house and went to a small room off to the side, going down two steps into the trading-post room. Nellie and Archie ran that store for many years, and it proved to be an immense help to the families at Shungopavi, who no longer had to make the long trip to First Mesa to make their purchases.

Nellie's basket is still talked about on the mesas, and her little store is often remembered. But the more lasting part of the story is that Nellie always told the children of her village that if they tried and persevered, they could accomplish anything that they set their minds to. Hadn't she, a nearly penniless Hopi, created the largest Hopi basket ever made? Hadn't she created it with just her own hands and skills? Even today, people in Second Mesa tell her story as an inspiration to young people to never give up, to follow their dreams.

*"CEM on mule at Polacca." Carey Melville (actually on a burro) is behind the Baptist church and the community building and laundry. The buildings at the center and the right utilize a masonry style that many young Hopi men learned while attending the Phoenix Indian School. The building to the left shows the old, traditional style.*

After their visit with the Quamallas at Coyote Springs, the group drove farther south to Polacca Wash. This large wash forms the drainage for First and Second Mesas. It is normally dry, but quickly becomes a raging river during the time of the summer rains. It drains into the Little Colorado River near Leupp. At the time of the Melvilles' visit, the wash was still running from heavy rains of the previous days. Margaret, the young Hopi girl, got too close to the water and fell in, but thankfully, the water was not deep and she was able to climb out with a bit of help. The families visited with an Indian man in the area, and he cut some yucca for Maud. He explained that the root of the yucca plant was used by the Hopis to make soap; it is also used for washing hair in certain ceremonies.

That night, Maud sat in the darkness and watched the stars appear over the mesa. She saw the headlights of three cars as they slowly climbed the narrow, dirt road up to the mesa top. There were a few lights moving on the mesa-top villages, and dogs barked in the distance. Maud marveled at the amazing sights she had seen throughout the day. She had a deep and growing awareness that she was in a special place. It was not just that it was different from the crowded urban cities in the East—she sensed the ancient, compelling aura of the mesas. There was a mystical and indefinable feeling that penetrated to her soul. That night she wrote in her journal, "Sky lovely, stars brighter than I ever saw."

The next morning Sellie brought more of her newly fired pottery. Maud especially liked Sellie; she thought she was "so sweet." Sellie was the name given to her by the missionaries after she began to attend church services. She was an older woman who lived in a tiny stone house just above the church and next to the water tower. Her house was between the houses of the sisters Ethel Muchvo and Hattie Carl. Sellie had one child, a daughter who lived in another state, so she depended on help from her neighbors, as well as the missionaries, although she was extremely self-sufficient for an older, single woman.

While Maud shopped for pottery, Carey worked on Abigail Johnson's car and patched the tires. Around mid-morning the Melvilles drove over to Second Mesa to visit with some basket makers. Maud met a woman named Omawu and ordered one of her unfinished baskets that they planned to return and pick up the following day. Carey photographed the villages on Second Mesa, as well as an old man riding a burro.

The following morning (Saturday), Maud did her family washing at the church laundry, and visited with Ruth Takala and her young daughter Loretta. Maud also bought some of Ruth's pottery. After the washing, the Melvilles went to the day school for a tour. Maud was impressed with all of the Hopi drawings that she saw displayed around the rooms. After the school visit, Maud and Martha went to Ethel Muchvo's house for a lesson in pottery making. With a great deal of Ethel's help, Maud finished her pot—and gained a great respect for the art of the Hopi potters.

*"Polacca School Room."* It is interesting to note that nearly all of the teaching materials and visual aids use traditional Hopi images, except for the picture of the Anglo baby on the clipboard, a teaching aid for the letter "B."

When Maud and Martha had finished their pots, they joined Carey and drove over to Second Mesa to get the basket. On their arrival in Shungopavi, Maud learned that Omawu had gotten up at dawn to finish it. She had worked on it steadily until the Melvilles arrived at seven that evening. For her day's labor, Omawu was paid five dollars.

The next day was Sunday, and the Melvilles attended services at the Baptist church. In the month of June there would have been many traditional cere-monies and kachina dances in the Hopi villages; however, the Melvilles attended none of them. Partly, this was out of respect for their official hostess,

Dorothy Humes, the missionary at Polacca, and aunt of young Maud's friend. But another likely reason the Melvilles did not attend ceremonies is that beginning in 1921, the Indian commissioner, Charles H. Burke, was on a campaign to stop the ceremonies in all the Indian pueblos in New Mexico and Arizona. In the Bureau of Indian Affairs regulations, the "Religious Crimes Code" stated that "all similar dances and so-called religious ceremonies, shall be considered 'Indian offences'" punishable by imprisonment. The Indian commissioner at Keams Canyon had complete power to jail Hopis for any reason. Many traditional Hopis were incarcerated, and without lawyers and formal charges and hearings, the Hopis had virtually no rights at that time.

Freedom of religion, which most American citizens enjoy under the Bill of Rights, did not apply to Indian religions. It was government policy to aid missionaries in converting Indians to Christianity. Hopis who converted were often rewarded with a government home (below the mesa), jobs and food, clothes, and other benefits that came through the churches. Those who became converts were called "Agency Indians," a statement of contempt from the more traditional Hopis. Even though Christian Hopis were still in the minority, there existed very strong pressure to leave the old Hopi ways behind.

Government officials also made it very difficult for visitors to the mesas to meet any Hopis, other than those who were "Christian converts or of proven loyalty to Indian Bureau policies." Given the wonderful range of Carey Melville's photographs of daily life at Hopi, the lack of a photograph or a reference to any ceremonies in Maud's journal is a conspicuous omission. The few tourists who traveled to the mesas often went with the goal of attending one of the amazing and compelling summer ceremonies. The Nimantikive (Home Dance) and the Snake Dance, in particular, brought many curious people to Hopiland.

But the Melvilles did see another part of Hopi life: they saw people going about their daily life, carrying wood, making baskets and pottery, and running out to the fields below the mesas. In many ways, Carey's photographs and Maud's observations on Hopi life are especially valuable as historic recordings. While many tourists recorded the kachina ceremonies, few documented daily life and work.

The Melvilles attended church services on Sunday, June 26, with about fifty Hopis. After church they had chicken dinner with Ethel Ryan and Dorothy Humes. Then there was another meeting in the afternoon, after which they walked up the steep trail to Walpi to hold a service. In the plaza, Sehepmana and then her husband, Hongavi, gave sermons. It had rained off and on all day, but when they went up to Walpi, Maud recorded that the sky was "marvelously lovely. Storms all about us but we were in sunlight."

After spending some time in Walpi, the Melvilles walked back down the trail to their camp. Along the way Maud gathered salt weed, which she cooked for supper. She stopped by Ethel Muchvo's house for a visit and met her uncle, Seventewa.

The Melvilles had planned to stay at Hopi for only a day or two, but as they met more people, their visit stretched to eight days. In a letter home, Maud wrote that she realized that every day they stayed at Hopi made them later and later, but she wondered "how can we leave when such a rare opportunity is ours. We are the most fortunate people on earth I believe." Maud truly felt blessed to have been able to see so much of Hopi life and to meet so many wonderful Hopi people. The first sentence in her letter summed up her feelings for Hopi: "*Never* in my life have I been in such a place."

Even so, the summer rains were coming in earnest, and they were warned that they should begin to pack and leave immediately, or the roads would become impassable, and they could be stranded at the mesas indefinitely. On Monday Carey spent most of the day packing the amazing quantities of pottery and baskets that they had purchased. Well over one hundred pounds of pottery, baskets, and kachinas were shipped back to Massachusetts. "C. packed pottery all day," Maud wrote. The Melvilles packed, but Maud wrote that it was hard to concentrate because every direction she looked there were rainbows—complete arches, doubles and triples. Storms were circling the skies, and Maud noted that they had five different rains, but she only saw the beauty of the vast arching heavens stretching forever over the mesas. "Sky lovely." She added that on her last evening at First Mesa, she could barely cook or eat "for running to see the rainbows."

All day Monday storms blew across the skies, drenching everyone. Ruth Takala came by and brought them some parched corn. And Maud went for one last visit with Ethel Muchvo, whom she had especially come to like. The two families, the Melvilles and the Muchvos, shared a last meal together at Ethel's house.

Maud did not sleep well that night. In the night the rain poured in torrents, and there were "3 gals of H2O" in Bob's corner of the tent. Through the dark hours she worried about getting "out." Even though the Melvilles were nearly packed and planning to leave, they were awakened early Tuesday morning by Ethel Ryan, who told them that she had spoken with Mr. Hubbell, the trader. He said they should leave immediately. The summer rainy season had begun, and with the violent storms there was a very real chance that they would be trapped by flood waters.

*Ethel, Minerva, and Clifford.*

Mr. and Mrs. Womack came to say goodbye, and Ethel and Wilfred Muchvo and their children Clifford and Minerva came to the Melvilles' camp. Ethel brought gifts for the children, and Wilfred gave Carey a stone hatchet. Another Hopi woman, Cora, came by with some pottery, but "in view of C's threat (!) I dared not buy." Abigail Johnson called from Second Mesa to inquire about the

*Grace Bancroft, a Baptist missionary, with Wilfred and Ethel Muchvo's children—*
*Clifford, age three, and Minerva, six months—and Martha Melville, 1927.*

Melvilles. Everyone hated to see the family leave, but they were also very anxious that they would be safely on their way before the anticipated flooding. The dry desert washes can fill instantly with flood waters from distant storms. Roads would wash out, and arroyos would be very difficult, and dangerous, to cross.

The Melvilles left First Mesa in the late morning. The little dog, Piki, was shut up in the laundry, "howling her head off," so that she could not follow the car. All along the way they were "always looking back at Polacca & the mesa." A few miles south of Polacca they met Tom Pavatea's truck, and the driver told them that the bridge over the arroyo was washed out. He suggested that they try another, longer, route. At one point the car and trailer got stuck in the mud and everyone had to get out of Hubbub to help. Carey dug out the mud from under the car, and Maud and the children pulled weeds to put under the tires to give the car some traction. And then they all "*pushed.*"

In the late afternoon they came to a flooded wash that they could not cross. Seven Navajo men on the other side yelled over the sound of the rushing water that it was too dangerous to attempt. They said the Melvilles should go the other way, but that was not an option because of the washed-out bridge. So the family drove back a few miles and made camp on higher ground. They planned to wait until the next day before attempting to travel on. Maud was concerned because they were carrying very little food with them, and she wrote that they all felt sort of "hopeless & helpless." They saw the beautiful buttes in the distance, and a lone Navajo hogan a few miles away.

That night the winds came rushing across the desert. To Maud it sounded like many trains speeding toward them, closer and closer. The winds shook the tent so roughly that they thought it might rip to pieces, and the tent was nearly torn from the tie-downs. The shaking of the wind set off the Melvilles' "Thef-a-larm" connected to the car. But the noise did not bother Maud; to her, it sounded rather comforting, like someone was standing guard over them. When Maud heard strange noises, Carey took the flashlight and crept out of the tent to check on them. He found the dish towels flapping loudly in the wind. Later she heard rustling sounds that she believed was a rattlesnake crawling along the edge of the tent. The rattlesnake proved to be a piece of paper caught in the tent ropes. It was a long and anxious night of sleeplessness combined with Maud's regret over having to leave a place that had totally captivated her, and a people who were forevermore held close to her heart.

In the pale morning light the Melvilles had coffee, cocoa, and Ruth Takala's parched corn for breakfast. They continued south to the big wash, where they were stopped once again. "Well, here we sit," Maud wrote. The frogs were croaking and the winds were blowing in more rain clouds. A Chevy was stranded on the other side of the wash, but a group of Navajos with a team of horses pulling a wagon came along, and after much discussion and a promise of payment, they pulled out the Chevy, and then went to work on getting the Melvilles across the arroyo. The trailer was unhitched from the car and, with three men pushing and chains on the tires, they got the automobile across the wash. Then the Navajos hitched their horses to the trailer and, again, with several men pushing, they got it across the muddy water. Carey Melville paid the Navajos three dollars for their help. Before they got away, Tom Pavatea's truck came along, but when the driver tried to cross the wash, the truck got stuck in the middle. The Melvilles loaned their spare chain for pulling out the truck, and then went on their way before the rains began again.

Once through the big wash, the Melvilles still had to contend with mud and sand. Crossing a nearly dry arroyo, and still only halfway to Winslow, the car and trailer got stuck once again in the sand going up the steep bank. Maud and the children all got out and pushed. After much work and the "worst kind of slipping & pushing," they finally got up and through the sandy wash. They were all "*Dead* tired," but even in her exhaustion, Maud loved the beautiful views of the Painted Desert—"the buttes are *lovely* in color & weird shape." They crossed the Little Colorado River, which was at "flood stage." Maud described it as looking like liquid red mud. Two arduous days and eighty-five miles later, the weary family arrived at Winslow at 5:30 in the evening. There they camped for the night and restocked their food supply.

They left Winslow, heading northwest for Leupp. The three children thought they would be really on their way again, and when Carey turned

*Hopi children play on the walls and passageways at Walpi.*

off the main road for a dirt-road detour to see Grand Falls, they were a "dreadfully dark crowd in the back seat because we left main rd. but C & I kept on merrily nevertheless." At a stop at Leupp Trading Post, Maud bought a beautiful Navajo rug for eight dollars, and they got directions to the Grand Falls of the Little Colorado River. The directions proved to be too vague, because the Melvilles followed many dirt tracks that led to Navajo hogans, and "Navajos are not much for conversation."

When the family finally reached the falls, they were all glad that they had made the effort to find the site. They heard the river first: "We could hear it tearing away the banks with big reports like a gun." At Grand Falls, the often

*A Pahaana lady talks with a Hopi woman on one of the upper roof levels at Walpi.*

nearly dry, flat, and shallow Little Colorado River drops straight down into a chasm that leads down and down until it meets with the main Colorado River. For much of the year the falls are nothing but a tumble of rock ledges, but after the intense summer rains the falls become an awesome sight with torrents of raging, muddy red water. Maud believed that the falls were as impressive as Niagara. "Dark red-brown water—thick looking. Immense fall of water—so glad we came." After seeing Grand Falls, the Melvilles, having much trouble with the carburetor, limped into Flagstaff, where they camped at the city park. In the high altitude they nearly froze that night, but in spite of the weather and automobile problems, Maud again recorded her pleasure at the beauty of the landscape: "The moon back of [the San Francisco Peaks] was the finest crescent line I ever saw, like a silver thread over the tall pines & deep blue hazy S.F. Mts." She was looking at the snow-capped peaks that are the spiritual and sacred home of the Hopi kachina spirits.

_⟨◉⟩_

From Flagstaff, the Melvilles continued their long trip. They drove north past Sunset Crater, "rosy hue of red lava looks like sunset all the time. Lava & cinder covered rounded hills all around," and Wupatki National Monument, the ancient Hopi ruins, where it was "Hotter than—." As they drove north to Cameron Trading Post at the Little Colorado River they were "Still in sight of Moqui Buttes. They seem like friends & connect us with Polacca."

From the trading post they turned northwest toward the Grand Canyon. The road was steep and rough. Several times they had to get out and push, and once they had to unload half of the trailer to make it up an incline. Late that night they made camp among the "stones, cedar and cactus." At noon the following day they reached the Grand Canyon. "The greatest impression was the *quietness*. No noise, no confusion. Just the murmur of the wind & a few birds flying near, & a dear little red flower growing right out on the tip end of a rock." Traveling along the rim they drove through "fields of blue lupines & tall pines."

The family hiked down into the Grand Canyon, where it was 114 degrees at the bottom, and young Maud became violently ill from drinking too much

*On the climb out of the Grand Canyon, the Melvilles were so exhausted they would just collapse on the ground and lie in the middle of the trail until they had rested a while.*

"Bright Angel water." The hike out the following day was an ordeal for all of them. Thankfully, a park service employee came along and offered to take young Maud up to the top on his mule because she was still very ill from drinking the creek water. It took the rest of the family over twelve hours to climb out of the canyon.

Young Maud recovered from her illness, but her mother could hardly walk for several days, suffering dizzy spells and cramps in her hands and legs. However, the Melvilles would not have missed the Grand Canyon for anything. They had never before seen anything like the colors and the vistas they saw there; it was a "panorama of peaks & minarets, pinnacles & towers, castles in Spain & fairy turrets of glowing colors & high lights, shadows & clouds blended by a blue haze like on the highest mt. peaks & over all is silence."

After leaving the Grand Canyon they drove to Prescott (where Maud bought copper trays), then south to Phoenix, where it was 112 degrees in the shade. There they "saw 1st giant cactus," saguaros. (The saguaro is the largest cactus in the U.S. It can grow to a height of fifty feet and lives up to 200 years. The white blossom of the saguaro is the state flower of Arizona.) In Phoenix they saw beds everywhere. Because of the heat, people slept outside in their yards or on the rooftops of the houses. Here they heard the slogan, "Phoenix, Hell and Yuma." As they headed west to California, they all decided that the slogan was absolutely true. In San Diego they visited Balboa Park and crossed into "Tia Juana," Mexico, for an afternoon. Then it was the "turning point of the trip." From southern California the Melvilles headed north. Along the way up the Pacific Coast they visited Yosemite and saw the towering redwoods. Then up to Oregon and Washington, where they turned east, heading back to Massachusetts, and the completion of their grand tour of America.

## ETHEL AND MAUD

ALTHOUGH THE MELVILLES ONLY SPENT A SHORT TIME on the Hopi Mesas, the influence of those days lasted through their lives, with the greatest emotional impact felt by Maud. For the next decade, she corresponded with her Hopi friend, Ethel Salyah Muchvo. She also sporadically wrote to Ruth Takala and the missionaries at First Mesa. Maud and Carey returned to Arizona and visited the Hopi Mesas in 1935, and again in the 1950s. And for many years Maud gave illustrated talks on the Hopis. She studied Indian music and read every book on the Hopis that she could find. Her brief visits to Hopi country transformed this New England woman.

Strangely, though, Maud's journal ends after the family left California. The only notes about the rest of the trip were listings of miles traveled in each state, with a total of 17,671 miles for the entire trip, and another list of the camps where they stayed in the tent, "tent ups." In Massachusetts the family settled back into their old life. The children returned to school in the fall, and Carey resumed his work at Clark University. In later years the children spoke very little of their amazing cross-country trip. Perhaps the new sights and people had

*Before they left the Hopi mesas, Maud Melville and her daughter Maud posed for a photo with her Hopi friends, Wilfred and Ethel Muchvo. The Muchvos are formally dressed in their best clothes.*

broadened their awareness, or, as a clipping from the *Worcester Telegram* stated, "The children have been painlessly educated in the history, geology and geography of this picturesque southwest," but evidently none of them brought it up very often in conversation or remembrances.

Maud, however, was profoundly changed by the trip, and most particularly by the time the family spent at the Hopi Mesas. Initially, back in Worcester, Carey gave talks on "Seeing America, 17,671 miles of scenery, romance and thrills in a Ford Car and Trailer." Maud's talks were on "Indians of the Southwest," "Hopi Indians—the Modern Cliff Dwellers," and "Among the Hopi Indians of the Southwest." As Maud continued to study Hopi culture and music, her lectures evolved, and she continued to be an active and popular speaker for many years. She was in great demand with area clubs and churches, and in her notes her fees were listed as $7.50 for an evening lecture, $10 for slides and curios, and $5 for "curios alone or curios alone at our home or at a church or home." Maud often donated these lecture fees to the First Mesa Baptist Church. In the missionaries' letters there are frequent mentions of gratitude over the years for her gifts and donations to the mission church. She lectured frequently for the Massachusetts Indian Association, and she corresponded with Indian scholars and authorities, including John Collier, commissioner of Indian Affairs.

Maud corresponded with Ethel Ryan and the other missionaries on the Hopi Mesas, including Abigail Johnson and Bertha Kirschke, and she exchanged occasional letters with the Hopi potter Ruth Takala; but it is her ten-year correspondence with Ethel Muchvo that is the most poignant. The missives are revealing and remarkable. Maud's letters no longer exist, and there are several possible reasons why they were not saved. Hopi houses are small, and any extra space is generally given to storing the necessities of life; also, paper was scarce at First Mesa in those years, so perhaps some letters were used to wrap small items or even used to start fires. Additionally, sometimes when a Hopi dies, some of his or her personal belongings are burned, in the belief that

*After Ethel showed Maud and her daughter how to make traditional Hopi pots, Ethel Ryan became interested in learning. Here, Ethel Muchvo holds the results of their class. Miss Ryan is holding baby Minerva, and little Clifford stands between them.*

the smoke carries the essence of those treasured possessions up to the heavens, where it will reside with the spirit of the deceased. However, most of Ethel's letters to Maud were preserved, and they are not only a historical treasure, they poignantly portray one Hopi woman's joys, her sorrows, the hardships, and the sheer struggles she endured to survive in a harsh and unforgiving country. There are few, if any, other instances from the 1920s and 1930s of existing letters from a Native American correspondent, still living a traditional life in a remote, nearly untouched area. Ethel's letters to her "Dear Loving Friend" speak of her work, her pottery, her children, Wilfred's sheep, the corn. They tell of illness and death, no rain, no food, and, tragically, no corn. The letters also document her struggle to survive through Wilfred's long illness and his decline, caused by tuberculosis, and the dilemma of remaining a traditional Hopi, against the promise of help from the Christian missionaries.

Regarding Ethel's letters, it is interesting to note that in contrast to today's casual world, all of Ethel's correspondence to Maud is addressed to "Mrs. Melville." To those of us in the twenty-first century, it seems strangely formal that after years of correspondence, "Dear Mrs. Melville" never became "Dear Maud." But in those times, in the 1920s and 1930s and even later, across America, it was customary for even close friends to address each other with the more formal "Mr." or "Mrs." So Ethel's formal salutations in her letters had nothing to do with distance or class or status or culture; rather, it was at that time simply a typical form for addressing a friend, in person as well as in correspondence.

Ethel was born a Tewa in Hano Village on First Mesa, but her mother died young, and she was raised by a Hopi woman in Walpi. Her family name was Dukepoo, but her Tewa name was Salyah (pronounced sal-YAH), which means "Spider Woman says my granddaughter." Ethel and her sister, Hattie Carl, were members of the Parrot/Kachina Clan, and both were accomplished potters. Hattie is thought to be the first Hopi woman to sign her pottery. Her Hopi name meant Cloud Flower, and her signature was a Hopi rain cloud with a flower coming out of the clouds. It is not known if Ethel signed her early work, but after her marriage she signed her pottery "Ethel Muchvo." Some of the pots that she sold to Maud Melville still exist. These are marked "Sahyah" or "Ethel." (While Ethel did sign some of her pots, Maud often used pencil to write an artist's name on a piece of pottery, using a phonetic spelling.)

Ethel married Wilfred Muchvo, and they built a tiny two-room stone house on a hill below First Mesa. Because her mother had died years earlier, Ethel did not inherit her mother's home up on the mesa. That is the reason that Ethel and Wilfred, as well as Hattie and Edwin Carl, had to build their homes on the hills below Hano. Ethel planted fruit trees in front of her house, and she also kept a garden for her beans and squash and melons. The back of the house dropped off to a shallow wash, and in that area Wilfred planted corn. At the edge of the wash, Ethel fired her pottery.

Hattie married Edwin Carl, and their stone house was a little below the Muchvos' home, closer to the church. Edwin was a Christian, and he often interpreted at church services. After he became a Christian, Hattie followed him into the church because, as her daughter related, "a wife follows her husband." The Carls had a ranch about six or seven miles north of First Mesa on Wepo Wash, and Ethel and Wilfred often walked up there to spend a few days visiting. Ethel and Wilfred also walked up the steep trail to the top of First Mesa when they went up for the traditional dances and ceremonies.

Ethel and Wilfred had a long and companionable marriage, during which they had twelve children. Unfortunately, Wilfred was afflicted with tuberculosis. He lived for many years with this disease, having periods of relative good health along with times when he became very ill. In those periods, Wilfred would be too weak to leave his bed, and he spent days and weeks coughing and spitting blood. At that time, there was little anyone could do to treat tuberculosis, and it is still not uncommon among the Hopis, although now detection and treatment are aggressively pursued. In later years the government built a tuberculosis sanatorium for Hopis in Winslow, but in the 1920s there was very little that could be done to combat this terrible and highly contagious disease, and it was almost always a death sentence.

Although Wilfred and Ethel had many children together, they lost them, one after another, because of the tuberculosis. Ethel's babies were born healthy

*The ancient rock pillar seen through the shaded passageway is a sacred place to the Hopis. Sometimes it is referred to as Snake Rock or Flower Rock.*

and lived for years or at least for several months after their births. But they were young and small, and very susceptible to the illness, particularly since they lived and slept in the tiny house with their father, who daily exposed them to the disease. Of course, it is not that Wilfred was anything but a kind and loving father, but in those times, illness was simply a fact of life. The Hopis used their traditional medicines to treat sickness and injuries, but as with all peoples, sometimes acceptance is ultimately the only course.

Naturally, all families of that time dealt with illnesses that today can be treated and cured. In a fall letter, just three months after the Melvilles' visit, Ethel Ryan wrote to the Melvilles, telling of the sad death of William Robinson, the son of the Reverend Forrest Robinson at Keams Canyon. During their June visit, William and the Melvilles' son Bob had played together. That September, William had become ill very suddenly, most likely with "infantile paralysis" (polio), and had died after being sick for only three days. It was a very sad and unexpected death: "William was such a fine lad and they had built high hopes in him."

*Fields at Keams Canyon.*

When Ethel and Wilfred met the Melvilles they had two children—four-year-old Clifford and three-month-old Minerva. By fall, Minerva was showing the beginning symptoms of her father's disease. In the first of Ethel's letters to her "Dear loving friends," written in early September of 1927, she mentions that the missionary had come by to check on Minerva because she was not feeling well. Fortunately, she recovered—for a while. Clifford was a healthy and rambunctious boy; all he wanted to do was go out with his father to "hert [herd] sheep." As the summer turned to fall, the Muchvos were feeling optimistic about the coming winter. There had been good summer rains, and Ethel wrote that "Wilfred is going to get lots of corn—this winter."

The letters show a reciprocal pattern of sharing and giving between the Melvilles and Muchvos over the years. In her letters, Ethel often asks for a specific item from Maud. In her September 1927 letter she asked for a coat for Wilfred. This was a nearly impossible item to get out on the Hopi Mesas, but without much trouble, Maud could send a used coat, perhaps an old one of Carey's or one from another friend in their area. On her part, Ethel sent many gifts. She was a piiki maker and often sent packages of her piiki, as well as dried Hopi corn, to the Melvilles. She also sent pots, although she sometimes needed an advance of enough money to pay for the postage because the pottery was so heavy and expensive to ship. And Wilfred sent gifts to Carey. Over the years, he sent kachinas, a drum, a flute and other musical instruments, turquoise jewelry, his hand-woven Hopi belts, and other items. The Melvilles and Muchvos also exchanged news and photographs of their families. Maud sent photos of her children, and the missionaries took photos of the Muchvos that Ethel sent to Massachusetts. Carey also sent a small camera along with rolls of film and asked Ethel and Wilfred to fill it with photographs of people and places on First Mesa, and to return the film for developing.

Maud sent a Christmas box to Ethel in December, but it took weeks to arrive at First Mesa. Ethel wrote that after she got Maud's letter telling of the box of gifts, she went to the post office every day to see if it had arrived, but she eventually became worried that it had been lost in the shipping. Soon, however, there were other things to worry about. That winter there was an epidemic of measles in the village, and everyone became sick. Ethel Ryan wrote that so far, fifty-four people on First Mesa had gotten sick. In the Muchvo home, Clifford was the first one to catch it, then Minerva. In those years, measles was an extremely fearful disease, and many people, especially the very young and very old, died from it. But Ethel wrote that Clifford had completely recovered, and although Minerva seemed better, she was still keeping her inside.

Ethel was alone because Wilfred was away herding his sheep. There was just her and the children and "the old man." This elderly man was Seventewa, Ethel's uncle. In the traditional Hopi way, women owned their homes, and if a man had no wife to live with, he always had a place at his mother's house or with one of his sisters, or her daughters. In Ethel's early letters, there are mentions of her uncle, and the Melvilles had met Seventewa during their visit the previous summer. In her December letter, Ethel wrote that as soon as Minerva was completely recovered, she planned to send Maud a box of piiki and also a pot. But for now she was anxiously waiting for the Christmas box, "just wateing for it, every time I go up to the Post offet when the miel come I neve get it." Ethel was also looking forward to seeing the pictures that Maud had mentioned she was sending with the Christmas box. "We will be glad when we get the pictures too—this is all I guess I have to say. So good-night to all of you."

In her time, Ethel was somewhat unusual because she could read and write. Many Hopis attended school only for a few years, sometimes being forced to leave their homes and attend government boarding schools far away, even in distant states. Typically, in these Indian boarding schools their hair was cut, their traditional clothing was taken away, and they were given uniforms. They were required to speak English only; there was often punishment for speaking their native language, and of course it was absolutely forbidden to practice any aspects of their traditional religion. But Ethel did learn to write in English, and even though her correspondence contains spelling and grammatical mistakes, her letters have a timeless eloquence. Her simple words convey a mother's love for her children, a wife's concern for an ill husband, and every parent's worry about providing for his or her children through the long, lean winter months.

*"Village view." A group of Pahaanas (Anglo tourists) stand in the plaza at Walpi. The imposing rock in the center has always had a ceremonial significance to the Hopis. Earlier referred to as Snake Rock, perhaps for the Snake Dance performed in the plaza, today it is often called Flower Rock.*

Maud's box arrived before the end of the year, containing many gifts for the family, including toys for the children. One gift for Clifford was a "little bath robe." He loved it, and wore it as an overcoat, every day, everywhere he went. At Christmastime the missionaries held a party and passed out gifts to nearly everyone on First Mesa. The trader Tom Pavatea donated beef and oranges and apples to provide a huge feast to feed the more than four hundred people who came by the church for the singing and the gifts. He also drove up to the mesa and brought down seven elderly and blind people, so they could enjoy the festivities. The Melvilles had also sent a box of gifts to Ruth Takala and her family. Ruth's gift was a scarf, and in January she wrote to Maud, thanking her for the gift, and closing her letter, "I'm glad you had still remember us and we are still remember you all…I'm Ruth Takala." Even though Christmas was definitely not a Hopi holiday, it still was a time for Christians and non-Christians alike to gather for a neighborly celebration. For the missionaries it was also a time when they felt their connection with the many people across the country who had sent their donations to the mission churches. Missionary Abigail Johnson, from Second Mesa, was compelled to commemorate her holiday with a poem:

> *Under the sparkling Christmas tree,*
> *Stacked in piles were loads of cheer,*
> *Some drawn from boxes thro' the year,*
> *From North and South and East and West,*
> *The friends have sent their very best...*
> *Under the sparkling Christmas tree,*
> *Were wagons strong as strong could be.*
> *All made to use for jolly play,*
> *Just after merry Christmas Day.*
> *And dolls came out to take a peep,*
> *Yes, some could even cry and sleep.*
> *This is the picture you may keep.*

Ethel wrote to Maud in the early spring telling her that they were all well and happy. Wilfred said to say "thank you" for his coat. And Ethel thanked Maud for the toys for the children. She wrote, "every time when they play with there play-think Clifford ask who sent it to them. and I alwas tell him." She inquired about Maud's family, and said that Miss Ryan had mentioned that the Melvilles would be sending pictures; she was waiting to see those. Little Minerva had many teeth

*Miss Abigail Johnson, who spoke Hopi fluently, lived most of her adult life at First or Second Mesa.*

and could eat now. They had a little pet pig, and "Minerva is very fat just like here pig." Ethel added, "and I have still remmber your girl and boy, you know they make little potterys I have already burn them, and did not sent them out yet...and tell you [your] girl & boy I am going to sent there little pottery some time if I have money to meil with." She closed the letter to her friend, "well good-night...ansur soon because I alwast like to get a letter from you."

Tragically, little Minerva's good health did not last. She became very sick in March, and she died on April 26, 1928. She was just thirteen months old. The whole family was grieving, and Clifford asked about Minerva constantly. Ethel wrote to Maud just three days after they lost Minerva—she just wanted to tell her what had happened. She wrote of how sad and unhappy the family was. Ethel added a request for an old cotton blanket or comforter because Minerva had "taken our blanket." Tiny Minerva, just one year old, had been wrapped in the family's only blanket. Even today when a Hopi person dies, the burial is generally taken care of by the family. There are certain things that are done before burial, and sometimes there is a special place near a village where babies and children are buried. But it is still common for a person to be wrapped for the burial in a blanket, often a quilt that was made by a family member, rather than to use a commercial or homemade casket.

Later that summer Ethel asked Miss Ryan to send Maud a small pot that she had made for her, as well as the two pots that Martha and Bob had made the previous summer. Ethel had painted and fired them. Ethel Ryan wrote, "Poor Ethel, she still grieves over Minerva's going." And she mentioned that it would be a great help if Maud would send an old quilt or a blanket for the family— Ethel would be "so grateful to receive it." She also requested some stockings for Ethel, "size 9," and a coverall for Clifford, who would be five on July 19. Wilfred had been sick again "spitting up blood...he does not look a bit well." She mentioned that if Mr. Melville had any old clothes, Wilfred would be very grateful if they would send them out. In closing, she mentioned that there had been "*no rains*" and she feared that "the Hopis will have a corn famine."

Ethel Muchvo's August letter thanked Maud for the things that she had sent, and she wondered if they had liked the pottery and piiki that she had sent to them. She mentioned that she had gone to do the washing and when she returned home Wilfred handed her Maud's postcard, and she was "very glad and happy" to hear from her. Enclosed in Ethel's letter was a photograph of Ethel and Clifford standing in front of the stone community building at the church. Ethel is wearing a white dress with a shawl across her shoulders and a woven Hopi belt tied around her waist. There is a perceptible sadness that can be seen on her face, and her arms hang down at her sides, empty now with the loss of her little daughter.

Wilfred became ill again in the fall, but recovered enough by November to go out to herd his sheep. Ethel had not gotten a letter from Maud for quite a while, and she wondered "why you never write to me for long time, maybe you have forgot all bout us, and we never forget you." She had asked Miss Ryan if she had heard from the Melvilles, but she had not gotten a letter from them either. Winter was coming on, and in her letter Ethel asked Maud for some old clothes for Wilfred since he would be out in the cold with his sheep. Clifford was well, "the boy is grown nice." The Muchvos had killed their pig the day before, Minerva's pet pig. Since the weather was cooler, the meat would keep better. Ethel closed her letter, "From Ethel Wilfred." Ethel had one last loss that year; her elderly uncle, Seventewa, whom she had taken in and cared for in his last years, died of double pneumonia during the night on the last day of the year, 1928.

In April of 1929, Ethel wrote again to Maud, thanking her for the clothes she had sent. She told Maud that Wilfred was making a necklace and a ring for her, and that she would make her a pot; she just needed Maud to let her know how large she would like it to be—"how many inches long will I make it, and what color red or yellow, please tell me about it, when you write." Ethel wrote that she had sent Clifford to Sunday school, and at the Easter service, when the little girls sang songs, Clifford stood at the front of the room and held the flowers. Ethel went to see Clifford at church, but Wilfred did not attend; he would not go to the church. After the services, Ethel and Clifford had dinner at the mission house with Miss Ryan, "we have some egas [eggs] for dinner, my we have a good time on esther day."

Later in the spring, Maud became concerned because she did not hear from anyone at First Mesa for many weeks. After receiving a second letter from Maud, Miss Ryan answered that there had been a flu epidemic and eight adults had died. She did not mention whether or not the Muchvo family had also been ill. Ethel Ryan had been one of those who contracted the flu. She became very ill and developed lung problems, and had to go to Tucson, Arizona, for several weeks "to bake in the sunshine." After she spent time in the warmer desert climate she was able to recover from her illness.

In a poignant closing to her letter Miss Ryan added that she had given Ethel Muchvo the photo the Melvilles had sent of Minerva. This photograph was an enlargement of an especially nice picture of Ethel's baby girl. "Poor Ethel, she sat & looked & looked & then cried silently." The missionary offered to keep the picture at her house so that Ethel could look at it whenever she wished, thinking that it caused Ethel too much sadness to see it very often. But after looking at it a while longer, Ethel said she would take it with her. She

*Ethel and Clifford, August 1928. Little Clifford has grown taller in the year since the Melvilles' visit, but Ethel's somber face reflects the grief she still felt after the death of her daughter Minerva.*

took Minerva's picture home and hung it in a prominent place on her wall where she could see her darling Minerva every day.

Ethel did not make the promised vase for Maud that spring. Clifford became very ill. He had contracted tuberculosis from his father. He was sleeping all of the time, waking only occasionally to eat, and he became terribly thin. Miss Ryan wrote that "he looks like a famine sufferer." Ethel Ryan was also very worried for Ethel Muchvo. She had already lost ten children, and Clifford was her only child now. There had been plans a few weeks earlier to take Clifford and Wilfred to the East Farm Sanatorium in Phoenix. The doctor thought that there was a chance for Clifford to recover if he went there, but when he became so frail, they were afraid to have him make the trip. "He will be 6, if he lives until July 19th." She asked Maud to send a note to Ethel; she knew it would mean a lot to her to know that the Melvilles were praying for her boy.

There was also another struggle going on at this time, a battle for Ethel's soul. With Wilfred being so sick year after year, it fell to Ethel to provide much of the support for her family. She was able to sell her pottery to Tom Pavatea, and in trading pottery and piiki and other Hopi gifts with Maud, she was able to obtain clothing and other necessities. Gifts from the missionaries were also a significant contribution to the survival of her family, but of course, the price for those gifts was an expectation to follow "the Christian Way." Miss Ryan thought that Ethel had an interest in the church, but that Wilfred was holding her back. Hopis who converted suffered terrible censure and persecution from the Hopi families and friends who resisted Christianity. Christian converts were forced to leave their traditional homes on the mesa and were told to go and live below "with the dead" (a reference to the fact that Hopis buried their dead in the rocky hills and cliffs below the mesa). When Hopis converted to Christianity, in many ways they became "dead" to their traditional religion, to Hopi ways, and to their families. Christian Hopis lost access to the clan fields that provided the corn and crops that ensured their very survival. There were beatings and death threats, and one missionary even admitted that when a Hopi was baptized, their families often mourned for them as though they had died. But, on the other side, the missionaries demanded absolute acceptance of

Christianity and rejection of traditional Hopi life. If a baptized Hopi had a lapse, if he attended a dance or a ceremony up on the mesa, the missionaries meted out strong chastisement to the "fallen."

These lifelong battles for souls between the Hopis and Christians did not end with a person's death. Often there was a struggle with the missionaries who believed that a Christian burial with a casket, hymns, and words from the Bible was necessary to send a soul to "awaken in Heaven." Many families, on the other hand, believed that a traditional Hopi ceremony was required to send a person's soul to live with the kachina spirits, the Cloud People, who reside near the San Francisco Peaks and ultimately become the clouds that bring life-giving rains to the Hopis. A traditional Hopi was buried in a cere-mony—a "pagan ceremony," that, according to the missionaries, consisted of "putting a cotton mask on the face, placing a wreath of eagle feathers around the head and then cramming the casket with Hopi food, quilts, blankets, etc." In fact, according to Hopi tradition, no food or personal items are included in the burial, although some items may be burned. Of all practices, sometimes it was this last conflict between the traditional Hopis and the missionaries that was the most bitter for the living.

Ethel was caught in the middle of this struggle. It is not known if she had a true interest in becoming a Christian. She does not mention the church very often in her letters to Maud, although she sometimes tells of visits with Miss Ryan. In later years, Ethel seemed to be more connected to traditional Hopi life, although with the loss of so many children, perhaps the missionaries promised some solace from her grief. And once again, she faced losing another child. Clifford did not live to be six. "Clifford has gone." Ethel Ryan relayed the sad news to Maud that Clifford had died of tuberculosis on July 1, 1929, three weeks before his sixth birthday. Ethel Muchvo was overcome with grief, and Miss Ryan hoped that Maud would write to her soon to send her condolences.

It was a long, sad summer for Ethel. She had now lost eleven children (her twelfth child was yet to come), and Wilfred's health continued to go up and down. In September, Ethel responded to a letter from Maud, "The best friend," saying that she had been very glad to hear from her. Ethel mentioned that she had been doing the washing and ironing for the missionaries. She received $1.25 a week for working for Miss Ryan and Miss Bancroft. But they had gone back East for visits with their families, so now it was just Miss Bertha Kirschke at the mission, and Ethel was only getting seventy-five cents for doing her laundry.

Ethel Ryan had given a box of things from Maud to Ethel, including some lengths of fabric. Ethel Muchvo planned on stitching one piece into a dress for herself. There was also another silky piece that she would sew into a shirt for Wilfred. That was a nice surprise to get in the mail, but mostly she was unable to do much work; she had no energy, and her days were long and sad. Ethel was still mourning Clifford's loss, and she wrote to Maud that some days she just felt like crying. In her package Ethel included a bracelet and a ring for Maud, and Wilfred sent a "doll" (a kachina carving) for Carey. Ethel wrote that they were gifts to the Melvilles: "we don't want you to sell them away. Just remember us all the time. I and Wilfred will never forget you all." Through the loss of her last child, Ethel seemed to need to connect with her friend Maud.

That summer the crops were growing well, but then came heavy rains and Wilfred's fields of corn and melons were all washed away. Just a few weeks earlier, Ethel Ryan's niece, Mary Ryan, had been visiting at First Mesa. In her letter home she mentioned that they had walked to the wash one morning and it was deep and full of rushing water. She had seen many "interesting articles" being carried down the wash, including watermelons. Ethel wrote that they did have a lot of "piches" (peaches) on their trees up by the house, so she was going to try to "can them up." She added that she wished that Maud and Carey could come out and be with them and they would eat some peaches together. Her letter closed, "Your turely friend, Ethel Wilfred."

_◎))_

If life was hard for the Hopis, with too little rain, too much rain, illness, and government mandates, it was also difficult for the missionaries. They lived a spartan existence at the missions; running water and heat were luxuries. Transportation was difficult; walking was the most common means of getting around, unless they could get a ride from one of the traders (Abigail Johnson had a car, but it was not always reliable). Language barriers were a huge obstacle. There was also constant hostility from the traditional Hopis who resented the very presence of the "mission Marys." It was a stressful endeavor for these single women who came from radically different lives in Eastern cities.

In the fall of 1929, Ethel Ryan went home for a visit, and even though she was still a relatively young woman, her health was so poor the doctors would not allow her to return to the Hopi Reservation. She had lost so much weight, she was down to 115 pounds. She spent much of the fall at Hot Springs, New Mexico, bathing in the waters that, hopefully, would help her arthritis and rheumatism. She also underwent "electrical" treatments for her deteriorating joints. She then went to Phoenix to spend the winter, with the hope that the warmer climate would allow her to continue to improve and gain weight. When she went to Massachusetts to see her family, and also to visit with the Melvilles, she knew that the doctors wanted her to take some time off from her mission duties, but she was ashamed to admit that she would not be returning to First Mesa until the late spring of the following year.

Ethel Ryan was not the only missionary whose health suffered from the difficult work with the Hopis out on the reservation. Abigail Johnson, whose work at First and Second Mesa spanned three decades, was on the verge of a complete breakdown, and doctors had ordered her to take a year off from her missionary work. She went to New Mexico with Miss Ryan, then on to California, and did not return to Arizona for an entire year.

In her October letter to the Melvilles explaining her absence from First Mesa, Ethel Ryan mentioned that she had seen Ethel and Wilfred and that they were both well. She also wrote to Miss Kirschke, the missionary who replaced Miss Ryan at First Mesa, telling her that the Melvilles had requested that she take photos of Tom Pavatea; Ruth and her husband, Takala (also called Roscoe Takala); and Sehepmana and Hongavi (Ruth's parents). She had also told Ethel and Wilfred that Maud wished to have a photo of them, with Ethel wearing her traditional "Tewa costume." She wrote that Wilfred was planning on making some small kachina carvings that he would sell to them

*The trader Tom Pavatea in front of his store in Polacca, at the base of First Mesa.*

for thirty-five cents apiece. But, once again, Wilfred got sick that fall—"you know that kind of sickness he always gets." Times were hard for Ethel because their fields had been washed away, and with the missionaries gone she had lost an important source of income doing their laundry. And because Wilfred was ill, he could not herd his sheep or even make kachinas to sell or trade.

Maud had sent some fabric to Ethel to make a dress, but Ethel needed one additional yard. "It is a silky and it has flowers on it." She said that she would be happy to pay for it if Maud would let her know the cost. She also asked for a pair of old shoes for Wilfred, and she closed with "we sent our best love to you."

In late November there was a surprising one and only letter from "Mr. Wilfred" to Mr. Melville, dictated by Wilfred and written by Ethel. "I was sick, I am all well now, so I mask [make] you some dolls to sent it you." Wilfred had made six kachina dolls that he was sending to Carey, and he asked him to sell them for him. "I am going to ask you when I will make some dolls and sent them to you and you will sell them for me." In the package there was also one of Ethel's vases for Maud to sell, but she would know the price, "you know the pottery," and also some piiki, a gift for the Melvilles.

Kachina dolls have been made for centuries. They were traditionally given to a young girl or an infant, and they symbolically represented a prayer that she would be healthy and have a long life and many children. The wooden carved and painted kachinas given to young girls were simple flat dolls, and they were often given at the Bean Dance, Powamuya, held in February, or in the summer at the Home Dance, Nimantikive. In the late 1800s, traders and tourists began purchasing these carvings as souvenirs and art collectibles, and eventually, the style began to evolve into intricate, freestanding sculptures that signified various kachinas. Today there are between three and four hundred kachinas, representing animals, birds, and the many spirits recognized by the Hopis.

Wilfred would have made his kachina dolls from a piece of cottonwood root. The cottonwood has symbolic significance as a water-seeking tree that only grows near springs and washes, places where there is an adequate supply of water. The wood is soft enough that it can be carved with hand tools. Wilfred used a small knife to shape his kachina dolls, and perhaps a file to smooth the carvings, and a piece of sandstone to finish the surfaces. In early times, the figures were painted with natural mineral dyes such as kaolin for white, copper carbonate or malachite for green or blue, red from ground hematite, and soot or corn smut for black. These are also the substances the Hopis have used as body paints. Feathers, fur, beads, and leather completed the sculptures.

At the time that Wilfred was making his carvings it is likely that he only worked on them when there were no children about. Traditionally, the carvings were gifts from the supernatural kachinas. But over time, and with the demand from buyers, that taboo faded, and the dolls were created in the home, where the process would have been seen by children. Because the early kachina figures were gifts from the spiritual beings, they were not signed. Today the carvings are viewed as art, and most of the sculptures are signed, or sometimes a clan symbol used by the artist is drawn or carved somewhere on the kachina. None of Wilfred's kachinas are signed, although Maud sometimes made notes or penciled the name of the maker on a favorite piece of pottery or carving.

In December Ethel wrote again after she had received a letter from Maud. She had actually gotten Maud's letter when she went to the post office to send

Wilfred's letter and the package of kachinas. She inquired about Maud's mother, who had been ill. "I and Wilfred are glad your mother got well," she wrote, and she asked Maud to send her six yards of black fabric for a dress. "You know I don't make it like your dresses." She would make a Hopi dress, a *manta*, from the cloth, "but I have to pay for it," so she wanted to know the cost. A Hopi woman's dress is traditionally made of black wool, and in earlier times the fabric would have been made by a Hopi man, who would spin and weave the cloth using wool from his flock of sheep. Hopi men also traditionally would be the ones who would stitch the fabric into a dress for their wives and daughters. The manta is a simple tube-style dress that went over one shoulder, generally the right shoulder, but left the other shoulder, as well as the arms, bare.

Ethel also inquired if the Melvilles had enjoyed the piiki that she had sent to them, "in nice colors pink white and blue." Wilfred and Ethel had been staying up on the mesa, helping a relative who just had a baby girl. Most likely, Ethel was helping the new mother for the first days after the birth of the baby, when the Hopi mother is secluded inside the house with no visitors, eating special foods and caring for the baby at this time when it is most fragile and vulnerable (this practice continues today). At the end of twenty days there would be a naming ceremony, where gifts of quilts and clan names are given to the infant. The naming ceremony takes place just at dawn when relatives gather and ritually wash the mother's hair with yucca-root soap. Then the baby is washed, and sometimes white corn meal is gently rubbed on the child. Paternal aunts and their female clan relatives give a gift of a quilt and a clan name, and offer a blessing that the child will enjoy a long and healthy life. In earlier times the infant's father would have made a cradleboard for the baby, and he would likely also have woven a blanket to wrap the infant. By the 1920s, the missionaries had taught quilting to the Hopi women, and quilts soon replaced the hand-woven blankets as a favored gift for the baby. This ceremony is followed by a feast of special foods, including piiki and *pik'ami,* a traditional sweet corn pudding that is baked overnight in a pit oven.

Ethel explained that she and Wilfred would be returning to their home below the mesa. But it is likely that even this involvement in Hopi tradition would have been frowned upon by the missionaries. Ethel probably enjoyed helping to care for the new baby, but it also reminded her of Clifford, and again, she wrote that she always felt like crying when she thought of him. But

*George and Myra Lomayeswa. Myra, an early convert to the Baptist Church, was a Christian for thirty-four years, and served as an interpreter at the First Mesa Baptist Church. George and Myra lived in one of the five houses south of Polacca.*

in spite of her sorrows, "we are so glad because Christmas is coming." Ethel was a strong woman. She accepted her sorrows and was able to carry on with her life. She worked hard, caring for Wilfred when he was ill, grateful for the times when he was healthy.

At the end of December, Ethel wrote to Maud again, thanking her for the photographs they had sent, including some enlargements. She also appreciated the paper for writing (to Maud). From the missionaries they had gotten a box of candy from Miss Bancroft, a looking glass from Miss Kirschke, and one dollar from Miss Minerva. Ethel and Wilfred had gone to the church for Christmas to see the tree, but when they went home that night, Wilfred became very ill, coughing blood. "I don't know why he alwas have like that kind of sickes [sickness]." Ethel wanted Maud to tell Mr. Melville thank you "for make our picture large for us." And Wilfred wanted Ethel to thank Carey for the belt that he had given to Wilfred when they had first met more than two years earlier. Wilfred was "still having it yet."

In the package of photographs there was one picture that Ethel and Wilfred found puzzling: "we dont the who it was maybe its you or some-body. Wilfred went me to ask you about it." Ethel thought that it was Maud in the photo, but Wilfred said no, it couldn't be, "I am sure you are going to laught [laugh] at us." It is possible that in some of the pictures that the Melvilles sent to the Muchvos, they just looked so different in their Eastern surroundings, and wearing more formal Anglo clothing, that the Muchvos could not be sure who it was in the pictures. It had also been more than two years since they first met, so it is likely that the Melvilles looked very different in the photos. In this package, there were three enlargements of photos of the Muchvos, along with the "unknown" picture. In saying good-bye in her letter, Ethel added, "well Mrs Melville we never forget you all, and just remember us all the time and answer soon. I and Wilfred we said good-bye to you all, Your loving friends."

At the end of each year the missionaries wrote a Christmas letter telling of the holiday events. Christmas was a time when many Hopis came to the church, Christians as well as traditional Hopis. There was always a feast, and this year Bertha Kirschke had made up two large wash boilers of coffee. Tom Pavatea donated apples for everyone who attended, and his son Theodore gave a pair of stockings to each of the Christian women and a handkerchief to each of the men. Other gifts were given out as well. Before Christmas the missionaries went through the boxes of donated clothes and toys and made up bags to give to everyone. Suitable gifts of dresses, baby clothes, shirts, toys, and other gifts were allocated and labeled for everyone they thought would attend the Christmas events. George Lomayeswa, a Christian Hopi who lived at the five houses just south of Polacca, gave a Christmas message in Hopi. In their annual letter to Baptist supporters around the country, the missionaries asked for everyone's prayers "that many more of them [the Hopis] may come to walk in the Jesus Road."

Reverend Teachout in Keams Canyon had a similar event for the Navajos. Ethel and Wilfred had been invited, and Reverend Teachout asked her to make some bread. He was planning to pick them up in his car to take them to the church at Keams Canyon for the Christmas party. Ethel ground a big sack of flour for the bread, a chore requiring many hours of hand grinding with a *mano,* a smooth stone held in the hand. Today women use electric mills to grind their wheat and corn, but in Ethel's day, all of that work was done by hand, kneeling at a grinding bin. Unfortunately, after Ethel did all of that work, their plans to go to the Christmas party did not work out; "that night Wilfred he got sick, so we did not go that day so we are very sorry for that."

MISS ETHEL L. RYAN
POLACCA
ARIZONA

Feb. 24, 1930

Dear Mrs. Melville:

Bought the baskets with money you gave me last summer. Am enclosing in top basket in envelope 39 negatives which I wish you would return when you are through with them.

If Mr. Melville still has that negative of Mr. Womack's of woman making piki I wish he would have 24 made for me and I'll be glad to pay him.

We have been in strict quarantine since Feb. 12 — no church services a gatherings. There are 3 positive

## DO PRAY FOR US ALL

WILFRED WAS VERY ILL THROUGHOUT THAT WINTER. Ethel Ryan, meanwhile, recovered enough to return to the Hopi mission at the end of January 1930. She had gained twelve pounds. She wrote to Maud that Ethel Muchvo was very pleased with the three photo enlargements that the Melvilles sent to them; those were the photos of Ethel and Wilfred, and Ethel Muchvo had also shown Ethel Ryan the puzzling photo of the unknown person (it was Maud). Ethel Ryan was also sending thirty-nine film negatives for Carey to print for her, and she asked if he still had his negative of Wama making piiki. If so, she would like to have twenty-four copies of the photo.

Ethel Ryan wrote that there was currently a quarantine in effect because of an epidemic of spinal meningitis. Two babies had already died and there were three more positive cases. Because the Hopi villages were so compact, people lived immediately next to each other, and interaction was constant. As a result, contagious diseases were able to spread unchecked through the communities. And, given the fact that many of these diseases were recently introduced through outside contact, the Hopis generally had little natural resistance to them. Diseases such as measles, flu, and smallpox were especially deadly.

Ethel Ryan owed Maud a dollar left over from money she sent for buying and shipping Hopi baskets back to the Melvilles (a wicker basket from Oraibi was $2.50, and pottery ranged from five to fifteen cents apiece—generally, the shipping cost more than the goods being sent). But Ethel said that if Maud didn't mind, she would like to give the dollar to Ethel Muchvo because she had to pay that much to have the Melvilles' Christmas packages brought out from Holbrook. Ethel Ryan added that Wilfred looked bad, "bloated and yellow. He may live for years, yet, but I wouldn't be surprised if he went anytime." She added that Ethel Muchvo "is just wrapped up in him."

*A view of the southwestern side of Walpi on First Mesa. On the left side of the photograph a ladder extends up from the underground ceremonial chamber of the Antelope Kiva.*

It is interesting that Ethel Ryan commented on Ethel's devotion to Wilfred, as though it was unusual or unexpected. But Ethel was loyal to her husband; she obviously cared very deeply for him, and in spite of his years of illness, she never blamed him for infecting the children, if, indeed she knew the cause of their deaths. In her letters, she often writes of the times that they laughed together, and even though it often fell to Ethel to support and feed her family, she and Wilfred did seem to be a team, united and supportive of each other. Her feelings for Wilfred are very apparent through the years when she cared for him through his frequent bouts of illness due to the tuberculosis. When the Melvilles' daughter married, Ethel even wrote to her and gave her some marital advice. She told her to always be kind to her husband and always stay with him.

By February, Wilfred's health had improved, and Ethel wrote to Maud that he planned to make more dolls for Carey to sell. They had not had any snow that winter, but it had rained a little, and "Wilfred look better now." In a six-page letter she thanked Maud for the cloth that she had sent, as she had been so anxious to get it to make some clothes; she was in such a hurry for it that Wilfred had been teasing her about it. Ethel was glad that Maud was wearing the ring they sent. She had also sent a bracelet and pottery and some piiki, but she didn't want the Melvilles to pay for it. It was intended to be a gift. And in a deeply memorable passage in her letter, Ethel wrote that Wilfred said that he was going to make a drum to send to the Melvilles, "and Mr Melville will sing for you and you can dance." The significance of this passage is that Ethel and Wilfred always thought of their dear little deceased son, Clifford, and of how he had always danced. "We never forget our little boy, we alwas remember him wat he do, he alwas dance."

For the Hopis, music and dance have ancient spiritual and ceremonial connections. Ethel explained that Wilfred wanted to make the drum for the Melvilles because they were their best friends, and through the gift of a drum, they would be linking their very different lives. "Mrs Melville you are just the same like I am." In her simple words, Ethel reached across the years and the miles, across the barriers of language and culture, affirming that they were both just two mothers, two wives, and, much more, they were friends.

On her part, Maud also believed in the power of music. She believed that song was the connection between the Hopis and their sacred spirits. She believed that they truly heard the song of the sun and of the rains and the sweep of the wind through the canyons. One of Maud's lectures was on Hopi music, and she wrote pages and pages of notes on the significance of Hopi song, along with descriptions of Hopi lullabies, love songs, and chants. Maud collected Hopi songs from Ethel and Wilfred and others. She also asked Ethel and Wilfred to send her Hopi instruments. In addition to the drum, she collected a flute, gourd rattles with cottonwood handles, a rasp, and a resonator. The resonator is a gourd painted to look like a turtle; spots on its back represent raindrops. To play it, the rasp is placed on the back of the turtle, and then the rasp is rubbed with a painted scapula bone from a sheep. The unique sound of the rasp is sometimes heard at the Home Dance, Nimantikive, and is played by the Hemis Mana Kachina.

Perhaps Ethel told Maud of the Hopi lullaby wherein the mother lulls her child to sleep with the refrain, "*puwva, puwva*" ("sleep sleep"), and sings of the beetles sleeping on the trails. The beetles carry one another on their backs, like the Hopi mother with her baby wrapped on a cradleboard. Natalie Curtis, a young musicologist who visited the Hopis before 1921, made this translation: "In the trail the beetles, On each other's backs are sleeping, So on mine, my baby, thou, sleep, sleep, sleep." Maud loved to share the Hopi lullaby in her talks, as well as the song about the butterfly maidens chasing each other over the cornfields after the rain, also recounted by Curtis in her book. The Hopi songs that Ethel sent to Maud were another connection between the two women; when Maud gave her talks to the groups in the East, she was sharing stories of Ethel's life, her land, and her culture.

In her long letter to Maud, Ethel also told that on February 6, she had made some pink and blue piiki for Miss Ryan because it was her birthday. When she took the piiki over to the mission, she and Wilfred and Sellie had been invited to return for dinner with the missionaries. At dinner that evening, Miss Ryan asked Ethel the date of her birthday, but Ethel did not know it, so Miss Ryan said that they could both have their birthdays that day because they shared the same name. Naturally, in those early years, babies were born at home without doctors, and without an official recording of their births. It is not uncommon that older Hopis, even today, do not know their actual birth dates, because many do not have birth certificates. Later that evening they all decided that perhaps Wilfred and Miss Kirschke could also share a birthday.

Ethel added in her letter that Wilfred wanted her to thank Carey for the saw he had sent out. Wilfred was very proud of the saw, which he used to make his kachina dolls. "Every time someone come in here, they ask him where he get it, the Hopis and Tewa mans. He always say the friend of us sent it."

Ethel told Maud to watch for a package of her "dried peachers. Please don't pay for it." She always harvested them every fall, and she had also taken some to the missionaries. Centuries earlier, Spanish explorers had brought peaches

*Ethel, Wilfred, Sellie, and an unknown missionary having dinner at the Polacca mission, February 1930. The birthday dinner at the mission was a special celebration—there were even candles on the table.*

to Hopi country. The seeds were planted, and peach orchards became very common. At harvest time, the peaches were split open and laid on walls and rooftops to dry. Early photos show them all through the villages, thousands of peaches drying in the sun, spread out on exposed flat rocks along the escarpment of the mesa cliffs. Families had areas they used for this purpose, and they generally stayed with the peaches for several days until they were dried and could be gathered up. Ethel had been working on her pottery when the mailman came and brought her a letter from Maud. "I got this letter and I was so glad of it. Well I and Wilfred said goodbye to you and Mr Melville…Your loving friends, Mrs Ethel Wilfred."

Ethel wrote to Maud again at the end of February, telling her that she knew that she was going to have a baby, "I can fell it now." Ethel had been very sick with the pregnancy but was feeling much better now that the early weeks were over. She asked Maud to send some old clothes that she could use to cover the baby. She was also sending a photograph that she hoped Carey could enlarge, and when Maud knew the cost of the enlargement, Ethel would send payment for it. Even though Ethel always offered to send money for fabric and photographs and other items, it is rather unlikely that she was able to do so very often because very little real money was used on the reservation. Even when she was able to sell some of her pottery, Ethel generally only got a trade credit at Tom Pavatea's trading post. It would have been rather unusual for her to have been paid in cash. One reason for this is that, at that time, most transactions among the Hopis were a trade or barter in which people exchanged goods and services. But another reason is that the traders wished to confine the commerce to their own stores, and without cars, it was very difficult to travel to a larger store or town. Some traders gave out trade tokens—tin money, rather than cash—that could only be used at their trading post. That was one way that a trader could ensure that the people would continue to trade and buy at his store. But more often, transactions were logged into a ledger book with a running total of debt or credit to each individual.

It snowed a couple of inches at the end of February, but not enough to make a great difference. It had been a dry winter for the Hopis, and the little

*In one of her occasional letters to Maud, Ruth Takala included a photo of her six-year-old daughter, Loretta, taken in March 1930.*

*Kunaa was a very elderly, blind woman mentioned in Maud Melville's diary. Maud noted that they watched her grind corn at her home on top of First Mesa.*

snow that they had gotten had only made the roads and trails muddy. Ruth Takala wrote to Maud and sent her some parched corn. She also included a photograph of her youngest daughter, Loretta. She was nearly six years old and would be going to school in the fall. She mentioned that Piki, the puppy that the children had named and had played with during their 1927 visit, was a big dog now: "he stays on the mesa." Ruth added that they had had a very sad loss that winter: their oldest son, fourteen-year-old John, had died from appendicitis. They were all grieving over his death.

The meningitis quarantine lasted until March 6 and was lifted when there were no new cases, but was reinstated for another month when another case was discovered. Then it was extended again because of several more cases of the deadly disease. Miss Ryan sent a box to Maud that included a basket and four small pots that she had ordered. There were also gifts from Ethel—a large pot and three ears of corn. Ethel would have selected three perfect ears of Hopi corn as a gift for her friend, perhaps special ears of blue corn. Wilfred was doing a little better, but he "will never be well." Miss Ryan wrote that "Dear old Kunaa, our oldest church member & sister of Seventewa," died on March 9. If Kunaa was Seventewa's sister, she would also have been an aunt of Ethel Muchvo. Kunaa lived up on top of the mesa at Hano with her daughter, who was not a Christian. Kunaa had been very ill, and a few days before she died, she asked her family to tell the missionaries, and she instructed them, "don't bury me Hopi Way." When she died, Tom Pavatea and Ethel Ryan went up to the mesa in his car to get Kunaa. Inside her house, all the relatives were waiting and sitting on the floor around her. Kunaa's son-in-law had a prayer stick, a "pahoo-willow stick with an eagle's feather attached." He asked to put it in the box with Kunaa, but Miss Ryan told him no. Kunaa "walked the Jesus Way and was not on the old road at all, so she won't need that." Then Tom and Ethel Ryan piled her bedding and clothing into the car and brought Kunaa down in the back seat. Ethel and Bertha Kirschke then carried her into the Hopi room at the church, and they had her funeral the next day. Kunaa's quilt was used to line the coffin, a government-made box.

Ethel Ryan was very sad about Kunaa's passing. "I loved her and called her grandmother." Kunaa's white woven robes and belt, most likely her wedding garments, traditionally used in Hopi burials, were not buried with her; Miss Ryan kept them. She reminded Maud that she and Carey had met Kunaa on their visit up to First Mesa, and they had gone into her home and sung. "She was little, had grey hair & was blind." Ethel remembered the photograph that Carey had taken of Kunaa. She asked if he would make thirty-six copies of the photo, plus an enlargement for her. Hopefully, he could print them "at once," and Ethel would pay the copy and shipping costs.

In mid-March Ethel Muchvo told Maud that they had gotten the letter she sent with the money for the kachina dolls. Ethel had been at the church doing the washing for the missionaries when Wilfred walked over with the letter, and Ethel was so glad the money had come. She was grinding corn to help her relative: "I am grinding corn on money to help Lora Toby." (It is unclear if Ethel was buying corn to grind for the wedding, or grinding corn to earn money for the wedding, but either way, she did need the money to help with the wedding, and Maud's letter with the money for the kachinas was very welcome.) Lora Toby, her uncle's daughter, was getting married, and it was traditional for all of the family members to help with the event. Ethel wrote that she would be very glad to make more vases for Maud to sell, as Maud had requested in her letter. Tom Pavatea was not buying any vases, and "it is very hard for the Hopi to get money to buye there Flour and coffee." It was the Depression, and the financial impact had spread even to the remote Hopi Reservation. These were hard years for the Hopis, even though theirs was still mostly a cashless, bartering society.

Wilfred had not been able to make the drum for Carey, "and Wilfred said that he is very sorry for you because he did not make a drum yet, but he will make." He was having trouble finding the cottonwood, and a drum would require a large piece of the trunk. "So he is going to wind slow [Winslow, Arizona] for the cottoning wood [cottonwood] to make a drum." He also had to hunt for a piece of tanned horsehide to cover it. Wilfred had paid a man named Robert S. to drive him in his car to Zuni. He had paid him with two sheep. He was now going to get the same man to take him to get the cottonwood at Winslow, but now the man was asking for five dollars for that trip. Ethel also asked Maud about the pottery that she wanted. She wanted to know what kind of a vase Maud wanted and how large it should be.

Ethel needed to make some money because of her pregnancy. She planned on making some baby clothes, but she would greatly appreciate it if Maud would send some blankets. "I can make some baby clothers, and also we need blankets to. we alwas need every things when we are going to get baby." She also needed rubber nipples for baby bottles. Ethel was worried that this time, because she had lost so many babies, she would not have enough milk for this one, "and thank you Mrs Melville you are helping us all the time, you are going to help us again." Ethel was also sorry because Miss Ryan and Miss Kirschke were planning on going away again, "so they are paking there thinges." The missionaries did not take vacations; they left because the hardships of their lives and work on the mesas affected their health, and they generally went home or to a warmer climate to regain health and strength.

Five days later, on March 23, 1930, Ethel again wrote to Maud. She was sending twelve dolls and some parched corn. Wilfred made these dolls, and they were the same as before, thirty-five cents each. But he wanted the Melvilles to pick one out, if there was one that they liked, as a gift. The other dolls were to be sold and the money sent to the Muchvos. Wilfred had also made three dolls that were different, they were about eleven inches long. But he was not sending them. When Miss Ryan saw them she did not think that the Melvilles would like the large dolls; they were not the traditional small dolls that would be hung on a wall (or on a roof rafter in a Hopi home). So Wilfred took them to sell to Tom Pavatea at his Polacca store.

Ethel had been sick for some time. During her pregnancy, "about two monthly I did not get sick," but later that month she had a miscarriage and had to spend several days lying flat on her back. She had reportedly been the head person in a woman's Basket Dance and had spent a lot of time practicing in the kiva and then had danced for ten days. The disapproving missionary, Miss Ryan, believed all that exertion had brought on the miscarriage, and she always tried to persuade the Hopis not to participate in the ceremonies that she and other missionaries thought of as pagan. "Do pray for her. I know she is sorry for it all, and I cannot imagine what possessed her to do as she did."

When young girls are about fourteen years of age, they are initiated into one of the Women's Societies. The Lalkont and O'waqölt ceremonies culminate in Basket Dances that are held in village plazas. During their initiations, young girls are taken to the kivas, where they remain for four days. During this time they are instructed in the craft of making baskets, although they do not actually weave a basket or plaque during this time in the kiva. They do not weave a basket until they are initiated. They are also instructed on other things that a Hopi woman should know. At this time they are also given a ceremonial name and their hair is washed, a part of the sacred ritual. Although Ethel had her miscarriage in March, when it was reported that she had participated in a Basket Dance, the women's dances are traditionally held in the fall. Because fall has always been the time for the ceremonies for the Women's Societies, it is possible that the missionary was mistaken when she wrote that Ethel had participated in a Basket Dance. It is likely that it was a different ceremony, one that would have been held in the early spring.

Ethel Muchvo's next letter to Maud was short, just telling her that she had been ill, but was feeling a little better now. And that she was sending the kachina dolls and some parched corn. She wondered if Mr. Melville had been able to make the enlargement of a picture of her and Wilfred, and did Maud like the vase she had sent to her? And then she explained that she did not have time to write a long letter because Wilfred had killed a sheep that morning that she had to cut up. Some meat would be hung from ropes and dried like jerky meat, *sikwivutsni,* and some would be cooked. "This is all I have because I got sheep now. Your loving friend, Mrs Ethel Wilfred."

At the end of March, Ethel Ryan wrote another letter to Maud and sent her "3 Hopis" (dolls) that she hoped she could sell for Ruth Takala. Two of the fabric dolls were dressed in traditional Hopi women's clothing with a black manta. They each had a belt and a white shawl or blanket with stitching at each end, and white moccasins with wrappings that go up the leg to the knee. One doll was a maiden with her hair up in whorls, and the other was a married

*Ruth Takala and her mother, Sehepmana, in front of the laundry building, most likely during the Melvilles' 1935 visit. In her later years Ruth was a midwife. Her daughter Loretta said, "There were a lot of children around here named Ruth," in honor of her help at the births.*

lady with her hair gathered and hanging to each side of her face. There was also a baby in a woven wicker cradleboard that Ruth's mother, Sehepmana, made. Ruth was trying to earn money because she was building another house. She was asking seventy-five cents for each doll, plus postage.

⁘

Ethel Ryan and Bertha Kirschke mailed an interesting letter to their Christian supporters around the country in the spring, telling them of their work at First Mesa. Apparently they counted every person who attended prayer services (12), took sewing classes, and made visits to the laundry (2,343) and the baths (4,513). The missionaries had learned early that the best way to get the Indians to listen to their message was to somehow get them to come to the mission and then "the Word of God was given every time." Naturally, the baths and the laundry with the piped-in water would have been very popular with the Hopis, who had to carry every precious drop of water from the spring up the steep trails to their houses. Running water would have been a true luxury and would have appealed to anyone who had to use water so sparingly. And the sewing and quilting classes were also very practical. The missionaries provided the fabric, patterns, and sewing tools. They shared just enough cloth to begin a project or to stitch a quilt block. While the women, as well as the men, were sewing, the missionaries would read lessons from the Bible. And they would very likely return again to get more cloth to finish a garment or quilt at the next sewing class. One missionary told of her first week at the mesas. She was asked to hold the sewing class by herself. When all the women came in, she passed out enough cloth for them to make their quilts. But when she told the other missionaries how successful her class had been, they were all disapproving. She found out why the following week when she again held the sewing class—and no one came. When the Hopi women had all the cloth they needed to finish their sewing, they did not need to go to the church each week to get the material to complete a quilt.

The missionaries explained in their spring letter that there had only been five conversions in the previous year, but one of the Mennonite missionaries had translated the Gospels into Hopi, and they were hopeful that would result in more interest in the Bible among the Hopis. Ruth Takala's twelve-year-old son, Daniel, read the translations aloud very fluently. In closing, Ethel Ryan and Bertha Kirschke asked everyone to pray for Ethel Muchvo. It almost seemed that they realized how emotionally fragile she was with the loss of her eleven children, particularly with Clifford's death the previous summer, her miscarriage in the spring, and Wilfred's continuing illness. And in spite of her lapse in joining in the women's dance up on the mesa, the missionaries "have had many talks with her," and they were very hopeful that she was considering the Jesus Way.

In early May, Ethel Ryan wrote that the quarantine for spinal meningitis had finally been lifted at the end of April. But there was "a new foe in our midst." Measles had broken out, first among the Navajo children, at the Keams Canyon boarding school. It was a strange kind of measles, beginning with a hemorrhage from the nose and throat. Thirty children at the boarding school had the disease, three had already died, and eight more were seriously ill. The early years of government-mandated education were a true hardship, and often tragic for the Hopis and children of other tribes. Children were forcibly taken from their homes and their parents and carried far away to the government boarding schools in Phoenix or Kansas or California. Even Keams Canyon, at the eastern edge of the Hopi Reservation, was a tremendous distance for a family that had no transportation. When the children were taken to these boarding schools, they often did not see their parents and were not allowed to return home for years and years.

In the schools every attempt was made to eradicate the language, culture, and traditional religion of the children. But often the greater tragedy was the disease that the children were exposed to; most of these diseases were previously unknown to their people, and they had no immunity, nor were there effective treatments. Adding to the problem were the generally poorly staffed medical facilities at the schools, with few medicines and supplies available. In the crowded boarding schools, diseases spread unchecked, and many children died. Ruth and Roscoe Takala, the Melvilles' friends from Polacca, lost two sons at the Albuquerque school. Their oldest son, John, died after an operation for appendicitis, and their second son, Daniel, died in a flu epidemic that swept through the school and then turned into tubercular meningitis. Maud Melville wrote to Ruth inquiring about buying some of her pottery, but in her responding letter, Ruth explained about losing Daniel and wrote that she did not have anything to sell, she had not been making any pottery—"we have a big sorrow over us."

_◎)》_

Ethel Ryan left the Hopi Mesas in the summer of 1930 and went to Phoenix for a while to regain her health; she never returned to her work at the First Mesa Baptist Church. Ethel Muchvo missed Miss Ryan; the two women had been friends, and it was apparent that they had liked and respected each other. After Miss Ryan left First Mesa, Ethel seldom attended any of the events at the church. Abigail Johnson returned to First Mesa after her year off, but she was never as healthy or energetic as she had been before. Like many of the Hopis that she worked with, Abigail was afflicted with tuberculosis. She was being treated at a sanitarium in 1901 when she was offered the position at First Mesa. She left briefly in 1921 for health reasons and never enjoyed good health after that. Miss Johnson spent most of thirty-six years at First and Second Mesas, and in 1933 she wrote a book, *Beyond the Black Buttes,* about her experiences at the Hopi Mesas and her efforts to spread Christianity to the Hopi people. Surprisingly, in all her years at Hopi, Abigail never gained the slightest appreciation for Hopi ways. She had an intense dislike for the Hopi kachina ceremonies. Visitor Florence Crannell Means, in her book *Sunlight on the Hopi Mesas,* said of Miss Johnson, "She would turn her face away...rather than look upon those masked and painted and kilted monsters, the kachinas." She regarded the Hopis without Christianity as living in darkness and sin. Bertha Kirschke replaced Ethel Ryan, but only stayed at First Mesa for a short time. Then she also became ill and too frail to work any longer. Doctors ordered her to take an extended leave, and she returned to her family home in the East.

_◎)_

On June 1, 1930, Ethel's letter to Maud explained that she had not written for a couple of months because Wilfred had been so ill. "Wilfred got very very sick, he got sick the worse then he was. But he is little better now, so I am writing to you now." Maud had written to tell Ethel that her father had just died. And in her reply, Ethel wrote that at the same time Maud's father had been dying, Wilfred had also been very ill, the sickest that he had ever been. "So now I am so unhappy all the time, so poor me, Mrs Melville, I am haveing a harde time with this two man" (Ethel is referring to Wilfred and Maud's father). Even though her words are misspelled, Ethel eloquently relates that she knows the depth of emotion and sadness that Maud was feeling through the illness and death of her father. Through Wilfred's difficult sicknesses, Ethel very much understood the stress and heartache of watching a loved one go through a terrible illness.

On a happier note, Ethel was wondering how Maud liked the pictures they had sent. Carey Melville had given a camera to Ethel and Wilfred, and they took photos and sent the films to the Melvilles. Often, the Melvilles requested photos of specific people or activities. Then they would send copies back to share with the people who were in the pictures.

Ethel was very worried that summer of 1930. Wilfred had been too sick to plant, and Ethel was not washing for the missionaries because she had to care for Wilfred. Consequently, they had moved up to a home on top of the mesa in Hano where family members would help them. But the Muchvos were not the only ones concerned about the coming fall and winter; all of the Hopis were worried. There had been no rain, just terrible winds, and everything was drying up. "So I think the Hopi are not going to get any corn and mellon and no piches to." Ethel asked her friend to "ansure soon…I wish you will write to me to make me happy."

In the late summer, Ethel and Wilfred were still living up on the mesa. They had never gotten any crops because Wilfred was so sick. He had never been that sick before. "O yes Mrs Melville I have a heard time with Wilfred when he get sick, he got very very sick this year. I think he is going to die." He could not work in the fields and he could not herd sheep. Ethel wrote to ask if they would buy some kachina dolls because Wilfred was feeling a little better, "he is well now but he is not storn [strong]," and he was sometimes able to carve. And Ethel would also send some pottery if they would take it and sell it for them. "And also we say thank you for the money you are going to sent."

Ethel asked if the Melvilles had any old clothes or shoes they would send to them. Ethel knew they were in for a hard winter. The missionaries had left First Mesa, and Ethel wondered if Maud knew where Ethel Ryan had gone. She missed her missionary friend, but she had also lost a vital lifeline, a source of food and clothes and help for the times when Wilfred was ill. In the last lines of her letter, Ethel also mentioned that this was the very last of the writing paper that Maud had sent out to her. Even paper to write on was a valuable and fairly rare item at Hopi. Her letter ended, "when ever you want some things tell us so [we] can do it for you. well this is all I have to say. From your friend Ethel Salyah."

Maud and her husband were lifesavers for the Muchvos, with their help in selling carvings and pottery, and their gifts of fabric, used clothes, and shoes. Ethel wrote again in October asking if Maud would send some clothes for the winter. Wilfred was well enough to try to herd sheep, but he would be out in the "cold day." Ethel also wondered if Carey had ever been able to make an enlargement of the picture of the Muchvos and Sellie and Miss Ryan having their birthday dinner together. Since the missionaries had gone away it was very hard for them to get any money. But they were always so grateful for their friendship with the Melvilles. "I alwas say thank you when I put on my dresses, thank you ever so much…so please ansure this poor writing, and also Wilfred said good-bye to you. From your Dearst, Ethel Wilfred."

Two weeks later, Ethel thanked Maud for the box she had sent. "I am sure happy as can be and say thank you very much for the things you sent. we sure happy like bees." Wilfred had made some dolls, but they were the large ones, and Ethel was not sure if the Melvilles would like those. She wanted to know if they should send them. Wilfred was so pleased with his overcoat, "and lot of time Wilfred said thank and thank, and I did just the same to." They had moved back down to their house below the mesa, but as soon as he got the overcoat, Wilfred had put it on and walked up the rocky trail to the mesa "to let his mother see him." And Wilfred would be very happy to make a necklace for Maud (she had apparently asked about buying one). It would have blue stones in it, turquoise, "we call it Hopi necklace." They were so happy, and Ethel loved the dresses, too. They were just the right size for her, but too long, "so I have to make it short…and I always say thank you for this black & pink dresses, but you never here me when I say it." There was also a thanks for the writing paper and envelopes, and for the "little Ruster," a toy rooster. "It was so pretty, and we laugh at it, and thank you for all the things."

Gifts from the Melvilles were precious and very much appreciated by the Muchvos. The gratitude expressed in Ethel's letters was effusive and heartfelt, and Maud must have felt a glow in her heart, knowing that her simple gifts of fabric and paper and used clothes made such a tremendous difference in her friend's life. The Melvilles were comfortable, not wealthy, but their simple gifts, and their purchases of pottery and kachinas, sometimes meant survival to the Muchvos. Now that he was well, Ethel reported that Wilfred planned on searching for the wood to make the drum yet. He would send the large kachinas he had carved, and he would look for blue stones to make a necklace for Maud. Although she had not "burnt" it yet, Ethel had made pottery for the Melvilles, and also a piece for young Bob, a gift. After the pieces were fired, she would send them, along with a Hopi brush that Maud had asked for. The hairbrush, *nawuspi,* was made with a hand-sized bundle of stiff grass, cut flat at the bottom and tied with a piece of string or fabric. Maud saved the hairbrush, and later donated it, along with her collections, to Wesleyan University.

The missionary Bertha Kirschke also wrote to the Melvilles that November, even though she had not been at First Mesa when the Melvilles visited three years earlier and, consequently, had never met Maud and Carey. But she told Maud that she had gotten her check and cashed it, and, as requested, had given $4.00 to Ethel and $2.25 to Ruth Takala. The Baptists had just finished a two-week special campaign on First and Second Mesa. Ethel Muchvo had not attended any of the meetings. Miss Kirschke thought that she had possibly wanted to attend, but wrote, "I know Ethel was afraid to come to any of them, & looks troubled. Please continue to pray for her."

Ruth Takala also wrote to Maud to thank her for the money for her Hopi dolls stitched with fabric. Her mother had been pleased to hear from Mrs. Melville, and both she, Sehepmana, and her father, Hongavi, were well, but her parents were getting old. The fall and winter of 1930 was a very hard time for the Hopis. "This year is no rain and we have no corn. This year every thing is dry here." Without a good harvest, all of them would be suffering. And further on in her letter, Ruth wrote, "Hopis has no corn this year mebe get hungry that is why we are very sorry." Ruth was still mourning the loss of her sons, and she was sad and "very lonesome all the time."

The snows came in late November and Ethel wrote that it was very cold, but she and Wilfred were "well and happy." Ethel had fired her pottery, and she was sending a box to them that included a hat for Mr. Melville, a cape for Bob, little vases for "Miss Maud," and another vase for Martha, the "other girl I don't now how to spell her neam." She told Maud to look on the backs of the gifts because that was where she had written the names of the ones they were intended for. The Hopis were expecting a cold winter, "and we have cold warther [weather] out here, the snow was out here the frot [front] of my house, and it is cold out here."

A few days after Christmas, Ethel again wrote to Maud, telling her about their Christmas celebrations. Ethel had

*Ruth Takala's father, Hongavi, at eighty-two years old. Once a village chief and a Snake Priest in Sichomovi, after becoming a Christian Hongavi no longer participated in traditional Hopi ceremonies. At the time of their baptisms, Hopi Christian men cut off their hair, as long hair represented rain and all the blessings for which the kachinas dance.*

helped Miss Kirschke fill gift bags for all of the Hopis with toys and other items donated by church members in the East. Any money that had been sent was used to purchase some necessities, such as soap, to put in the bags. Wilfred had gotten a very special Christmas gift, a sheep: "and one man give Wilfred a sheep, and this sheep was tide to the chirstmas tree." Ethel hoped that the Melvilles had gotten the gifts that they sent to them. Did they laugh at the hat they sent for Bob? Wilfred had still not found any wood for the drum he planned to make, but they were going to send the necklace. It had been a lot of work for him; he had to go to the Zuni Pueblo in New Mexico to get the turquoise. (The Hopis have traditionally traded with the Zunis for turquoise and salt.) Ethel asked that

*When Sehepmana became too old and shaky to make pottery, she and her daughter Ruth made fabric dolls that they sold at the trading post or to the Melvilles.*

they let her know when they got the package, "and tell us when you get the beads so we can know it." She also thanked them for the enlargement of the picture from the birthday dinner they had months earlier at the mission house with Sellie, Miss Ryan, and Miss Kirschke, when they decided to share birthdays with the missionaries. Ethel wrote, "and thank you for ever things. and the picture was look nice."

Wilfred finished the necklace, as well as a bracelet, but they did not reach the Melvilles until the following February. It appears that the package with the necklace was mistakenly sent first to Dorothy Humes in Rhode Island.

Dorothy opened the package and was very impressed with the necklace. Apparently, Ethel and Wilfred were only asking five dollars for the set, and that was only to cover the costs of the beads. The Muchvos felt that the Melvilles had been so kind to them, such good friends, that they would not ask for the full value of the pieces. Dorothy explained in her letter to Maud when she forwarded the package that the turquoise alone would be worth nearly four dollars, and Wilfred would have had to go to the Zunis in New Mexico to get it. He would have had to take corn, or something to trade. There were also shells at the ends of the strings that are very rare and valuable to the Hopis. The shells with the red in them "are *very valuable*...to the desert people," the Hopis. "They really think almost as much of shell beads as of turquoise beads."

Shells were particularly valuable to the Hopis, partly because they came from such a distance from the mesas. Seashells generally came from the California coast, sometimes from the Gulf of California, and then they were traded from tribe to tribe until they reached the distant Hopi Mesas. Shells from California were traded inland, then to the Mojaves, the Hualapais, the Havasupais, and finally to the Hopis.

In a letter enclosed with the necklace and bracelet, Ethel had asked Maud to pick up any shells that they found and send them out to Wilfred. Shells that were thin and had a pearl lining could be used for beads. Dorothy Humes thought that the shells in the set were worth a dollar by themselves. So she assured Maud Melville that five dollars for the necklace and bracelet was a great price. Apparently, Maud planned on wearing them with a Hopi costume that she planned to borrow from Miss Humes and to wear when she gave her talks and presentations. Dorothy wrote that she would send the costume by the end of February. "I think the set is *great*, and adds quite a realistic touch to the costume."

Dorothy added that she had not thought of sending out shells to the Hopis, but it would be very easy for her to gather a box of them. Living in Rhode Island, she visited the beaches very often during the summers, and she planned on gathering a box of shells to send out to the Hopis. But then, on second thought, she decided to write first to some of the Christian Hopis to ask about shells and their use in ceremonial clothing. She did not want to do anything to further the native religion, and she would not send the shells if they were used "to make their ceremonial gowns more elaborate."

⟨◎⟩

In the spring of 1931, Ethel was expecting again. She would have an August baby. Dorothy Humes was appalled at this news. "That is pathetic! For Wilfred's T.B. condition will probably settle its fate unless it could have a very modern home and treatment right from the start." But she knew that with Ethel, "hope is always high in her heart when it comes to her babies." Dorothy did wish her well, and she hoped that the baby would live a long time.

Dorothy advised Maud to send some practical baby clothes. Colored percale dresses were easier to keep clean than white, and pink or blue would be pleasing. And baby blankets were especially treasured. A small blanket made of four thicknesses of grey cotton flannel, tied, or bound and quilted, was best. Quilts with cotton batting were more difficult to wash; they often got lumpy, so when Dorothy had been at the Hopi mission, she and Ethel Ryan had always made quilts with cotton flannel inside.

In other news, she wrote that Miss Ryan was still recuperating in Phoenix, and doctors had ordered Miss Kirschke to take a six-month leave for her health. The Melvilles were talking about making another visit to the Hopis, and Dorothy hoped that there would be someone they knew at the mission; it would be much nicer for them if there was someone there who they were familiar with. And if there was no one at the mission and the Melvilles sent money for kachinas or pottery, Dorothy advised, they should just send a postal money order to the Muchvos. Ethel and Wilfred knew about money orders, and it would be easy for them to cash one right there at the post office.

Ethel was very pleased about her pregnancy. She wrote to Maud in early February, asking if she had gotten the necklace; she hoped that it had not gotten lost in the mail. Ethel had not been making pottery because she was "going to get a baby, so that make me so weeks all the time, so I am not working on anything." Since Ethel could not make any pottery, Wilfred was "working heard on the dolls to make our living." Ethel wrote that he was "making some dolls to shell [sell] then to get out things to eat. he is working harde on the dolls." As pleased as she was about her pregnancy, Ethel often thought of all the children she had lost. "Just think of it how many chrienden I have lost and I just am going get [another] one." She prayed for the future of this baby, "I wish it will live all the time."

It is hard to fully imagine what Ethel would have been thinking about the prospect of having another baby, considering she had lost all her other children. In the 1930s, there was not much she could have done to prevent another pregnancy, nor is it likely that she would have wanted to do so. She was clearly happy to be carrying another child, and it shows her strength and optimism that she would look forward to the birth of her twelfth child with joy. Many other women in her place might have been racked with worry and anguish.

Later that spring, Ethel wrote that she was feeling very well, and said that the baby would be born in August. She also asked that Maud think of her and the baby in that month. The actual wording of her letter seems to ask that Maud would send her prayers to the new baby. Ethel was pleased that Maud had asked for some of their things. Wilfred had four dolls and would make two more, and since Ethel was feeling so well, she planned on making some pottery. She would make some vases for Maud. That would be very helpful for her because, once again, Tom Pavatea was not buying any pottery at that time. Ethel said that she was also fairly sure that she could get a woven Hopi belt for Maud, but the Hopi dress would be a bit more difficult. Ethel said that such a dress would cost twenty-five dollars, an astronomical amount for the Muchvos. The traditional Hopi dress, a manta, was usually hand woven from black wool. Evidently, after borrowing Dorothy Humes's Hopi dress, Maud decided to obtain one of her own that she could wear when giving Hopi presentations.

Sometime that spring, Maud had also written to Ruth Takala to inquire about buying her pottery, but Ruth had none. Ruth did send two of her fabric Hopi dolls, and her father, Hongavi, had made some kachina dolls that they sent to Maud. She closed her letter, "I am your friend, Ruth Takala."

At the end of April 1931, there was a last letter from Ethel Ryan, who was leaving Arizona for good. She had never completely regained her health, so she went one last time to First Mesa, just to gather up her things before she went back to her home in the East. She saw her old friends there and had a last visit with Ethel Muchvo, who told her about her baby expected at the end of the summer. She was so happy and hopeful about the baby, Ethel Ryan hoped that all would be well for her, as well as for Wilfred and the baby.

In her letter, Ethel Ryan also inquired about the "fair"—"Hope the fair was a great success. I know your Navajo rugs added much." Maud apparently worked with M. W. Billingsley to put on a show and sale of Southwestern Indian arts and crafts in central Massachusetts. Billingsley was an Arizonan who spent a great deal of time on the Hopi Mesas and came to know many Hopi people. In 1926, when some religious groups were trying to petition Congress to pass laws prohibiting the Hopi Snake Dance and kachina ceremonies, Billingsley organized a group of Hopis and took them to Washington D.C., where they performed a version of the Snake Dance, with live snakes, on the Capitol steps in front of members of Congress. Ultimately, efforts to ban the traditional ceremonies were dropped.

In later years, Billingsley became a great showman and took his group of Hopi ceremonial dancers across the country, to colleges and museums, to the 1939 World's Fair in New York, and even into Mexico and Canada to perform for various dignitaries. His Hopi friends helped to build a replica pueblo building for Billingsley on land he had homesteaded east of Mesa, Arizona, on the old Apache Trail. From that location he ran the Hopi House Trading Post and organized various events, called Arizona Indian Expositions. Billingsley called himself "The Only Authentic White Chief of the Hopi Indians."

There is no surviving information about the Indian fair in Massachusetts, but there is a fascinating group of photographs of the fair in the Melville collections. There are photos of Billingsley and his wife, Edythe Sterling-Billingsley. In the exposition brochures she is referred to as the historian and hostess of both the exposition and the trading post. In the photos she wears jodhpurs and cowboy boots, silver jewelry, and an enormous cowboy hat. Billingsley wears a conventional suit and tie and a hat. Several Indians also appear in the photos, but none of them look like Hopis. The fair consisted of large, open tents with

*M. W. "Billy" Billingsley and his wife, Edythe Sterling-Billingsley, organizers of the Arizona Indian Exposition. All Hopis who studied this image agree that the men on the right and left are not Hopis, although some thought they may have been from an Eastern tribe.*

tables covered with Navajo rugs and silver, along with a staggering assortment of exquisite Hopi pottery and kachinas and baskets. In the photos, New England matrons in heels and hose and gloves and hats look over the artwork.

⚭

On August 3, 1931, in the last week of her pregnancy, Ethel Muchvo wrote to her friend with a plea for help. She had not heard from Maud for several months, and Wilfred said "maybe you have forgot all about your Hopi friends." Ethel had some pottery but had not been able to "burn" the pieces, and Wilfred had been so ill that he was not able to do any work, so she could not ask him to fire her pottery. Things were desperate for Ethel and Wilfred. They had almost no corn left, and Ethel did not know how "we will be getting along with our living when the baby come."

Ethel wrote that soon after she had her baby she would be able to make more pottery to send to Maud, but very soon she hoped that Maud would send some things to help with her expected child. She again needed some old clothes to make diapers and baby gowns, and she especially needed a bottle and some nipples, because she did not think that she would be able to nurse the baby, "because I also have harde time for milk." It is not unlikely that Ethel and Wilfred were literally on the verge of starving. They had no crops, no corn; Wilfred was very ill, and if Ethel had little to eat, naturally she would not be able to provide much nourishment for her baby. Ethel's letter was a desperate plea for help from her friend. In closing she added, "Well, Mrs Melville please ansure this poor letter…ansure soon if you can." She signed it, "Your loving friend Ethel Wilfred."

Three weeks later there was another letter from Ethel. She wanted to tell her friend Maud about the new baby. Vivian had been born on August 9, after a very difficult and long delivery. Ethel was surprised because none of her other pregnancies had been that hard. But the baby was well, and Ethel was getting stronger every day. A box of things from Maud had come a few days after the baby's birth, and Ethel was very thankful for it, also for the money that she sent. Ethel wrote, "she is a girl and her neam is Vivian and her father is very happy with her." The box from Maud included some candy, but Ethel had not eaten any of it. She was on a restricted diet until some time after the baby's birth, likely until after the period of twenty days when a naming ceremony would take place. But Wilfred had enjoyed some of the candy. He was feeling stronger and was out with the men dipping sheep. Ethel asked Maud to tell Mr. Melville about the new baby; she knew that they would be glad to hear of little Vivian's birth.

Ethel's October letter told Maud that the baby was getting big, but Wilfred had asked her to write to ask for some old winter clothes, "old shirt & coats because it is getting cold now." They had a little corn from the recent harvest, but "we did not have much." They had dried the corn to store for the coming winter. But in late November Ethel had still not heard from Maud. It had been snowing steadily for several days and nights, "it was very very cold out here." The snow was over two feet deep. Ethel had sewn a tiny pair of shoes for the baby using some soft sheepskin. Little Vivian was getting strong and fat "like the pig," was already trying to turn over, and was also trying to hold things. Ethel wrote, "we are so happy with our little girl." In closing, she asked again if Maud would please try to send out some old clothes; most important, they needed a coat and some shoes for Wilfred.

At the end of the year, there was a thank you note from Ruth Takala, thanking Maud for the package she sent, and especially for the dress for her youngest child, little Loretta. There was also a six-page letter from Ethel to "dear loving Mrs Melville," thanking Maud for the things she sent. "We are as happy as can be when we get our things that you have sent it out." Ethel was wearing the dress that they sent, she had already shortened it (being one of Maud's old dresses, it was, of course, too long for Ethel), and Wilfred was wearing his shirt. Vivian was playing with the toy dog Maud sent to her. It was one that would bark, and when Wilfred made the dog bark for Vivian they all laughed. Ethel was so happy because Vivian was well and happy all the time, and, as she wrote to Maud, Wilfred was singing to Vivian, and she was holding her little dog.

Ethel wrote that there had been terrible, deep snows, and people were having a hard time. The animals were dying because they could not dig through the snow to find feed. Wilfred lost one of his sheep, "so we are very sorry for that," and Edwin Carl, husband to Ethel's sister Hattie, lost ten sheep. They had also heard that some Navajos living out in isolated hogans had died from the cold and from being stranded, "so we are afride of the snow." Ethel had made some vases to send to Maud, but the snow was too deep to fire them, and Wilfred had carved some of the large kachinas, but he could not go anywhere to sell them because the roads and trails were all impassable. She hoped that soon he would be able to get to Tom Pavatea's store to sell them because they were out of sugar and other necessities. "What a bad snow we have out here. I guss its going to snow again it look like it."

They had all gone to the church at Christmas, and after the singing, they had all gotten gifts, and "the little girl [Vivian] was laughing all night." One white man there was so charmed with Vivian that he told Miss Kirschke that she must give her some of the candy. They also gave Ethel some baby dresses, and everyone got some candy. Ethel thanked Maud again for all of the wonderful things they had sent out, the clothes for Wilfred and Vivian. Ethel had given one of the dresses to her sister Hattie, "my sister ask me for one dress, and I give her one. I guess that is all I have to say." As she looked outside, Ethel thought it looked like it was going to snow again.

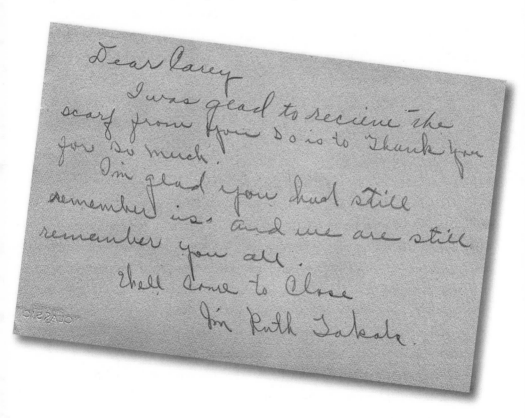

## YOUR LOVING FRIEND

AFTER 1931, THE LETTERS SEEM TO HAVE TAPERED OFF to fewer communications each year. In 1932 there are only four surviving letters. In March Ethel wrote to her "Dear best friend," thanking Maud for the clothes that she had sent to them. "The first think I have to say thank you very much for the things you sent." Wilfred "is so glad of his shirt. ... I am writing to you again. I haven write for long time and we are happy with our little girl." Little Vivian was seven months old, and she could sit up alone. She loved the rattle, and she held it all the time. She was also wearing the little coat from Maud, "and the little girl was so happy all the time...and she can sict up, all along now, and yes Mrs Melville she is trying to say papa." Ethel very much liked the dress from Maud, but it had short sleeves and most Hopi women covered their arms. Even when they wore the traditional manta that just went over one shoulder, they would wear a shawl or blanket, sometimes called a "back apron," over their arms and shoulders. So Ethel asked Maud to look for a half yard of matching pink fabric so that she could take out the short sleeves and add long sleeves to the dress.

Ethel added that Wilfred was feeling well, and soon it would be planting time so he would be working in the fields. He had made some dolls but had not painted them yet. He had also made some Hopi belts. When the dolls were finished they would send them, along with the belts, to the Melvilles, "when we fine the money then we will sent this things." Ethel wrote that they had no money to pay for the postage. The traders were not buying any pottery, and there was no way for them to get any money until they could sell some dolls or pottery. In the Depression years there was no market for Indian crafts; many traders had a full inventory but no place to sell it, and many trading posts went under.

Later that spring Wilfred finally found the materials for the drum, and after he shaped the wood and stretched the hide, they sent it to the Melvilles in May. It had involved a lot of searching and work to find the materials and to make the drum: "and how hard time we have for a drum. ... This drum is made of the cotton wood tree and cover with the buffoe skin." Included in the box that the Muchvos sent were two baskets and a gourd rattle; the rattle was a gift for Mr. Melville. In her letter, Ethel added that they were so proud of little Vivian, she was healthy and "fat like a pig." To Ethel, who knew too well of lean times, having a plump little daughter was a sign of health, of having adequate nourishment. In those times, being plump or fat was often a sign of wealth and abundance, while being thin reflected a scarcity of food, hard times, and starvation.

*Wilfred and Ethel Muchvo.*

When Wilfred packed paper into the box for shipping the drum, Vivian came along behind him and pulled out all of the papers and dropped them back on the floor. "And I am going to tell what this little girl did, her father Wilfred was going to pag [pack] this things, and he put the papers in the box, and this girl take all the paper out form the box." Vivian could sit up all alone, she could say "papa," "she has got two toote," and she loved to eat cookies and apples. Vivian was a precious child and an absolute delight to her parents. Ethel's letters to Maud are full of stories about Vivian, and over and over she writes about how happy they were to have their daughter. Perhaps that is one reason why Ethel's letters tapered off as the years went on; she was much more focused on raising Vivian, and she obviously was deriving so much joy and happiness in being a mother.

*Hattie Carl and Ethel Salyah Muchvo holding her baby (thought to be Ethel's last child, Vivian).*

Ethel wrote to Maud on August 9, 1932, Vivian's first birthday. It had been a hot, dry summer. Wilfred and the other Hopi farmers had planted their fields, but without any rain, nothing had come up. Ethel and Wilfred were very worried about the future: "Wilfred plant some corn and walterlom but they have not thing on it because they are all dry, and Wilfred is sorry for it because we have a girl, and we has no Green Corn." But little Vivian was healthy, she was trying to stand on her own, and now she had "6 toots." Ethel asked if they had gotten the drum and rattle they had sent, and Wilfred wanted Ethel to ask

Maud for some old clothes, especially stockings and socks. Ethel Ryan had been out for a brief visit, but she went back to her home in the East. "And Miss Ryan said, I wish Mrs Melville see this girl. I wish to said Wilfred."

Two weeks later Ethel wrote that she was sending some pictures of her family to the Melvilles, "I am sure you will be glad of it." One photo showed one-year-old Vivian sitting at the door playing with her kachina doll. Inside the house you can see the stove and Wilfred's beads hanging on the wall. Ethel and Wilfred used a camera and film provided by Carey Melville, and the missionaries had the film developed using money sent by the Melvilles. Since there were only a few trading posts on the mesas, the film had to be sent away to a larger city, sometimes even out of state, for developing. Then the finished prints were returned by mail. Over the years there was an ongoing exchange of photos, and there are frequent mentions in Ethel's letters of how the Melvilles looked and how their children were changing and growing. Times were still hard for Ethel and Wilfred. In closing her letter, Ethel wrote, "it is hard for us to get 3 cent stamp. Ansure soon if you can. Your loving friend, Ethel Wilfred." Perhaps the expense of paper and postage was another reason for Ethel's less frequent letters. In addition to the expense, there was also the difficulty of obtaining paper and pencils. When you had no crops, buying anything but food would have been out of the question.

Ethel wrote again two months later. She had apparently not gotten a letter from Maud for some time, because she asked once again if they had gotten the drum and rattle. With the poor harvest, all of the Hopis had been struggling; even the children were suffering, and many were becoming thin and listless. Vivian had been ill in the summer and had grown very thin. Ethel prayed that "Vivian will be fat again." And of course, she always feared that Vivian would become ill like her father and suffer the tragic fate of her first eleven children. Ethel asked again if the Melvilles would try to send out some old clothes, and Ethel hoped that Maud would write to her, "I always like to here from you."

Maud did get the drum that Wilfred made. In a November article in the local *Gazette* in Worcester, Massachusetts, there was a small notice: "Exhibits Ancient Indian Tom-Tom." Maud gave "an illustrated lecture on the Hopi

Indians" for the Old South Congregational Woman's Association. The brief clipping mentions that the drum that Maud exhibited, "an ancient Indian tom-tom," was given to her by a Hopi friend, Salyah. Salyah was Ethel's Hopi name, but the drum was not ancient; it was the drum that Wilfred had made that spring.

Ethel's next letter was dated July 5, 1933, nearly a year later. The Muchvos had all gone to Keams Canyon to the "July ground" for the Fourth of July celebrations. They wore the clothes that Maud had sent them at Christmas. Ethel wore her dress, Wilfred wore his shirt, and Vivian wore her yellow dress, "and sure she was look nice." There had been foot races. People ran for pottery vases; there were races for all categories—men, women, boys, and girls, and even one for "the white mens." Vivian was growing well, she would be two the coming month, and she often went up to spend time on the mesa with her grandmother, Wilfred's mother. After the races on the Fourth of July, Vivian had been taken up to the mesa to see her grandmother. Then Wilfred went up to get her and stayed so late, they had to walk down the trail after dark.

Later that summer, Maud sent some money to Ethel because she wanted to purchase more pottery, as well as a flute and a Hopi belt. Maud wrote that their son Bob was getting married soon, and they were sending out a new camera for Ethel and Wilfred. Ethel was glad that she had sent some money; she put it aside and would use it to pay for the items and shipping costs when she got everything together for Maud, "I am still keeping this money yet." Things were going well for their family. They were all well, even Wilfred had not been sick that year, and there had been rain that summer. Wilfred planted some corn and melons, and they were hoping for a good harvest. Ethel asked Maud to send some fabric for a dress that she could sew herself. She wanted a kind of dark fabric that would not fade. She closed her letter, "well good night Mr & Mrs Melville, from your dear loving friends, Ethel S. Wilfred."

In early September, Ethel wrote that she was sending a belt, the kind they called a "red belt, this belt we alwas ware." Wilfred had made the belt, and if they wanted another kind, he would make a black one. Not all Hopi men knew how to weave these traditional belts like Wilfred. Ethel also sent some gifts in the box: there was a plant for "Mrs Maud" (as she called Maud and Carey's daughter, the younger Maud, as she got older), and for Maud there was "the boule and vase and little spoon and the belt is to you." Two-year-old Vivian had painted the spoon, which was wrapped in paper and packed inside the vase, and Ethel knew that Maud would laugh when she saw it. The plant and pottery were gifts, but if Maud wanted to sell the belt, she should ask ten dollars for it.

Ethel hoped that Maud could sell the belt and send out the money because there had been a great tragedy with their crops. Their neighbor had nine cows, and they had gotten into Wilfred's field and had eaten all of their corn. They initially thought that the neighbor would pay for the damage, but they could not make him give them any money for their loss. "That day we are so sad about it. I thought we are going get lot of corn this year but not." So, once again, Ethel and Wilfred faced a lean winter. In earlier times, the Hopis mostly raised sheep, but the government encouraged them to go to cattle. As there were more problems with cattle wandering into the fields, the villages organized to build fences to keep them out of the crops. Unfortunately, there was no help for the Muchvos that fall.

They had been so hopeful about their corn; there had not been good summer rains, just enough for the Hopi corn, and Wilfred had worked diligently, tending the corn in the field. *"Trail up First Mesa."*

And while Ethel was writing to Maud it began to rain harder than Ethel had ever seen it rain. Her little piiki house was full of water. But even a heavy rain was a blessing to the Hopis. Little Vivian was "very happy as can be." She was outside in the rain playing with her kachina dolls. Ethel and Wilfred were also enjoying the camera that the Melvilles sent to them. They had a little trouble understanding how it operated. Wilfred turned the film before he took the pictures, so they ran out of film very quickly. But Miss Kirschke explained again how to use the camera, and Wilfred took it over to Second Mesa to take pictures of the Buffalo Dance. "And he forgot what Miss Kirchke said, and he turn it again befor he take it, and when he came back home and he was telling me, and I was so mad at him, but now we understeen how to use it and yesterday Wilfred take the old grandma picture with her husband."

## IT IS GETTING COLD OUT HERE

LIFE TOOK ANOTHER DOWNTURN for Ethel in the fall. She wrote, "I always think of you, Mrs Melville," and she hoped that the Melvilles had gotten the things that they had sent, and as she wrote nearly every fall, she added, "it is getting cold out here." Then she wrote her worrisome news, "Mrs Melville, I am going to tell you what Wilfred did. he sell all the sheeps, and O he made me so sade and unhappy all the time, when I go to bed I alwas think and think in the night how can we get long." But he did not sell the sheep for money. Wilfred sold all of his animals to get the "things that they ware when they dance." Wilfred had made a choice to return to a traditional Hopi life, to return to the mesa to participate in the religious kiva ceremonies and kachina dances. Without the sheep, everything would be hard for the family, especially with winter coming. Ethel explained to Maud that usually they could sell a sheep and get some money to buy the things that they needed. Now they had nothing. It was cold, and the snows would be starting soon.

Once again, Ethel asked Maud if she would be able to send out some old clothes and shoes because "my shoe and dresses are getting old." Ethel wrote that she was very mad at Wilfred, and she had many sleepless nights where she worried about how they would exist through the winter. And then Vivian asked for some meat, but "I don't now what to do with her, and she was crying and I cry with her."

Ethel had sent the woven Hopi belt and some pottery that Maud had requested in an earlier letter. Ethel also sent some pictures that they had taken with the camera the Melvilles sent to them. Since she had not heard back from Maud, she wondered if everything had arrived, and if they liked what she sent. She also asked if young Maud ("Mrs Maud") liked the pottery that she had sent especially for her, as a gift. And had Maud been able to sell the belt yet? Ethel knew that Maud was selling the pottery and kachinas that she sent; it was one way in which Maud could continue to keep buying from Ethel. Most likely, Maud sold the Hopi arts to friends and at her many talks. So, many of

*"Wood carrier." He is carrying* suwvi, *four-wing salt bush, traditionally used in the kivas. It is also used to heat the pit ovens out in the fields for roasting corn.*

the pots and vases and kachinas that Ethel sent back East were intended specifically to be sold, all except for the pottery that she sent unsolicited, which was meant as a gift. Ethel was pleased to tell Maud that Vivian was happy all the time, and asked her please not to forget to send the "winter coldes." She also asked that Maud send the money when she had sold the belt. Ethel closed her November letter, "ansure soon, your loving frend, Ethel Wilfred."

Ethel's letter to Maud on January 1, 1934, contained many thanks for the things that they had gotten from the Melvilles for Christmas. The shirt was too small for Wilfred, but the coat fit him and he was "glad of his coat." Ethel was pleased with the "dress good," the fabric to make her dress, and Vivian loved the toys. Vivian was well and happy, "and she can sing, and she talk to much, she made us laugh and she alwas want to do some thing." Ethel wrote that Vivian was always busy, doing things and playing, and she could even grind corn. The weather had been warm and dry, no snow, no rain. Vivian always played outside; she took all of her toys out to play in the winter sun, and she would sing as she played. Ethel had sent more film to the Melvilles—did they get it? They were anxious to know how the photos had turned out. "And Mrs Melville we want to know about our picture how Wilfred take it. When you write tell us about it...thank you very much. Your loving friend Ethel Wilfred."

Three weeks later Ethel wrote again, this time with a request for seven yards of "velvety" cloth. Ethel and Wilfred had been up on the mesa visiting her brother, Choyou, and because he knew that Ethel was good friends with Maud, he asked her to inquire if she would be able to find some velvety cloth, "brick-red." They needed so much fabric because Ethel's brother's wife, Helen, was a "very fat lady." "My brother said, he want you to tell us how much was the Velvety dress goods cost, he want it for his wife and this lady was very fat lady, so they want know how much will be 7 yard, so please tell us how much it will take for 7 yard, and they are going to sent you the money for that goods." Ethel told her brother that she would write to Maud because "she is my best friends and we love them very much." Ethel did not want Maud to send the cloth until they knew the price, but if she could hurry and let them know, they did need the "velvety goods" right away.

Ethel also mentioned that she and Wilfred were trying to write the words and music to the Hopi song that Maud had asked them for. Ethel was trying to get the words right in Hopi and in Tewa. Vivian was also helping because she would always sing along with them. Ethel wished that they had a phonograph to help to record the music. She thought that they could sing into it, and then send the recordings to Maud. "Wilfred said that I wish we have a phonograph he said and I said just the same I wish to, and Wilfred again if we have it then I will sing in to it, and we will sent the Records, then they can have lots of Hopi songs." Ethel was excited because she had gotten the news that the Melvilles were planning a trip to Hopi in the coming summer.

Ethel wrote to Maud again in the spring. Her brother's wife had not yet decided on the velvety cloth—there was discussion about getting the dark red, or possibly blue. Such a purchase seemed to need much consideration. Ethel was sending a roll of film. "Wilfred take all the pictures in it, and see how they will be done." She hoped that some of the pictures would come out well. They now had no more film, but they still had the camera. It had been a dry winter, with no snow, and no rain. But as Ethel wrote there was a huge snowstorm; the snow was already eight inches deep on the ground. Ethel was "so mad when it snowing," knowing that it had killed all of their peaches and apples. The weather had been so mild, the fruit trees had all flowered, and some Hopi farmers were already planting. They were still working on writing out the Hopi songs. Wilfred was carving kachina dolls, and Vivian was singing, "she was happy as can be...tell Mr Melville Vivian is the happy little girl."

Young Maud married Alfred Arnold in the spring of 1934, and when she learned of the wedding, Ethel sent some things to the young couple, most likely some of her pottery. After the wedding, Maud sent a wedding photograph to Ethel and Wilfred. Ethel thought that "Mrs Maude" was a "nice looking lady you are. you have your wedding dresses on." Ethel wrote a letter to Maud Arnold that included some advice to the new bride: "I am glad for you when you get merring. So be king (kind) to your man. and be with him all the tine..." She wrote that they should try to be best friends with each other. Some of the Hopi women did not stay with their husbands, they went with

*Ethel's sister, Hattie Carl, 1927, in front of the church at Polacca. She wears formal Hopi women's clothing and a silver squash-blossom necklace that today her daughter proudly wears to church on most Sundays. Behind Hattie is First Mesa, with the round water tower to the right and the home of Sellie, the potter, to the left.*

other men. But not Ethel, she was "with my one husband yet…so we must try hard to be nice to them Mrs Maude if we can."

The Melvilles had talked of making another visit to the Hopi Mesas that summer, but apparently the plans had not come together. Ethel asked Maud Arnold if she had heard any news of a trip from her mother. "And your mother said that they are coming out here again, so we are waitining for then. and they haven come yet. plase talk to your mother. and ask her when they are coming out. and they mush tell us when they will come." Ethel said that she hoped that the Melvilles would be coming out, and when they did, they would sing Hopi songs together: "and they mush tell us when they will come, and tell her we will make the song out here if we can." Ethel also asked young Maud to ask her mother, if they were coming, would she be able to bring some of her old stockings? Ethel had been mending her stockings over and over, and there was not much left of them. So she would very much appreciate some of Maud's old stockings and any other old clothes that she might have.

It is very likely that the Melvilles did not make the trip to Arizona because of the responsibilities and activities related to their daughter's wedding. But they did have Hopi guests in June. A clipping from the local Worcester paper, the *Gazette,* stated on June 20, 1934, "Hopi Chieftains are Guests at Luncheon Here." M. W. and Edythe Billingsley were traveling with six Hopis when they stopped in Worcester. The paper stated that seven years earlier the Melvilles had traveled to the Southwest and became friends with a Hopi woman (Ethel Muchvo) with whom they had corresponded regularly. Two of the Hopis, Slaoftoche and Kolchoftewa, were friends of Wilfred Muchvo, the Hopi woman's husband, and they "were luncheon guests at the Melville home, 16 Isabella Street." The article went on to state that while they were in Massachusetts "the Indians present a version of the [snake] dance, using real snakes."

Earlier in the year, Maud had sent out a box that contained some candy. Ethel's brother Choyou had been at their home when they opened the box and had been greatly impressed that they had such great friends who always sent them many wonderful things. He knew of some other Hopis who had Pahaana friends, but none of them ever received such nice clothes and dresses. Choyou said, "you has the nice good best friends you has." Ethel knew very well that Maud was her "nice good friend." She wrote, "we remember you all the time, never forget you."

Sometime that year, the Muchvos met "one white man" who began taking them to Indian Wells, a trading post about forty-three miles south of First Mesa on the road to Holbrook. They went in their friend's truck. In Ethel's December 2 letter to Maud, she told her that they had been to Indian Wells six times that year. Indian Wells trading center was housed in a large stone building, originally built by the Richardson family and later owned by Babbitt Brothers Trading. In early times it was a way station for the stagecoach line. Ethel does not mention in her letters whether the man who drove them to

Indian Wells was a missionary or, more likely, a trader. They would camp out when they got to Indian Wells and usually would return the following day. Ethel was making a lot of pottery that she sold there, and Wilfred was carving dolls to sell.

The family was excited because their Pahaana friend said that when they went to Indian Wells on their next trip they would celebrate Christmas there. Ethel was making more pottery to sell at that trading post, and Wilfred was painting some kachina dolls that they planned to send to the Melvilles. Little Vivian was very excited about the approaching holiday. Ethel wrote that every night before she went to bed she asked if the "santclass" would bring her a little toy piano, so they were trying to get her one. Ethel had been very glad to hear from her friend Maud. Neither of them had written for several months, but apparently they had both written at the same time and their letters crossed in the mail. "I am very glad to here from you, and you did just the same, I did."

Wilfred sent his regards to Mr. Melville and asked if it would be possible for him to send another small saw. The one he had given to Wilfred a few years earlier had broken. They still had the camera that Carey sent to them, and Ethel said she would send the latest film for developing. A few months earlier Wilfred took the camera up to the mesa and took photographs of a Butterfly Dance. But then he left the camera up there at his mother's house, and one of the children opened it and played with the film, so Ethel did not know how the photos would come out. "And I was so mad at him, and I say to him, my we are just wasting it, they are cost lot of money, I say to him, and I am sorry for that and I don't now how it will come out when we sent then."

Ethel wanted to know what Mr. Melville had asked the "santclass" to bring him. Vivian wanted the little piano, and Ethel dreamed of having a phonograph. When Vivian asked her papa what he wanted, he said some butter and a coat, "and he made us laugh." Ethel asked Maud to tell Miss Ryan that she still remembered her and that she "sent her our best love to her." Ethel Ryan had moved back to the East. Her family lived in Massachusetts, not far from the Melvilles, and Ethel was staying with friends in Rhode Island. But she was still not strong enough to return to any kind of work. Ethel Muchvo wished that Ethel Ryan would write, but she had not yet heard from her after she left Polacca. She said that if Miss Ryan wanted any piiki, she would make some and send it, but she did not want her to pay for it. Ethel also hoped that Maud would answer her letter soon, and she closed it, "from your loving friends, Mrs Ethel Wilfred & Vivian."

Two weeks before Christmas, Ethel sent some of Wilfred's dolls for the Melvilles to sell. With the money they got for the kachina dolls she wanted them to send out a small saw or knife that Wilfred could use for his carving. Ethel just included a short note, "Hollow Mrs Melville, Wilfred is sending you the dolls." The prices were on the dolls; they were the same price that they got from Tom Pavatea. "I gust you will be glad when you get this dolls. From Your friend Ethel Wilfred."

―◎))

Strangely, there are no existing letters from Ethel or any of the missionaries in 1935. Given their frequent correspondence, it is very likely that Ethel and Maud did write, but for some reason, those letters have been lost over the years. But the Melvilles did make a visit to First Mesa sometime in the summer of that year, according to family recollections. Also, in the family's photo collections at least a dozen pictures are identified as having been taken in 1935. In contrast to the 1927 photos that contained many images of the mesas and villages, the 1935 photos are mostly of people. It is apparent that the Melvilles were visiting their old friends. There is Sellie, looking a bit older, with a grandson, Dale, wrapped in a blanket and carried on her back. There are several photos of the Muchvos who also look older, but very happy to be able to show off their adorable daughter Vivian. The smiling girl appears in four of the pictures. In two of them she has been dressed in her traditional Hopi dress, a manta, along with a Hopi woven belt and shawl, and white moccasins and wrapped leggings.

In the 1935 photos, Wilfred looks healthier than ever. He wears a turquoise necklace and a cloth tied around his head, and there is a broad smile on his face. Ethel has a serene look, but her face also shows the wear of the many hard

*"Sellie, 1935." Sellie is wrapped in a Pendleton blanket. All of the children loved Sellie. Her granddaughter Elsie remarked, "She was everything good to us."*

*Wilfred Muchvo standing in front of the Baptist church, the mesa skyline visible behind him.*

times and sorrows that she has borne. It is unfortunate that there are no surviving letters from the time of the Melvilles' visit. It would have been revealing to know the things Maud and Ethel talked of. Clearly their lives had gone in vastly different directions. Maud lived in her big Eastern house, a professor's wife, giving talks on the Hopis and studying Pueblo music. She belonged to many clubs; she was president of the Worcester Women's Club, the College Club, which later became the American Association of University Women, and the Clark University Faculty Women's Club. Her children grew to adulthood and married, and they all enjoyed successful lives. Ethel stayed in her tiny stone house, caring for Wilfred during the times when he became ill, planting her garden, hoping for rain but not so much snow, and making pottery to survive, all the while praying that little Vivian, her twelfth child and the light of her life, would not be stricken with the dreaded tuberculosis that had taken all of her previous babies. Very likely the two old friends talked of their husbands and children, their families, and their daily work. Perhaps they sang the Hopi songs together.

_☽_

The film from the Butterfly Dance that Ethel mentioned in her 1934 letter was not mailed for more than a year. The missionary, Bertha Kirschke, sent it in March 1936, along with another roll of film. She had waited so long because she did not have the Melvilles' address in Massachusetts. She had taken photos of Ethel and Wilfred and little Vivian, as Maud had requested. Later that summer Bertha again wrote and said that she hoped to take more photos of some of the church members that the Melvilles had met, but George Lomayeswa had been in the hospital for the last two weeks, and his wife, Myra, had also been sick. So Bertha planned on waiting a while until everyone was feeling well, before taking their photographs for the Melvilles.

The missionaries had been very busy that summer because they held a series of special evangelistic services, presided over by a visiting preacher, Jim Smith. They had remodeled the laundry and made it into a community building, and it was waiting to be repainted. Nearly seventy adults and children had attended, including a woman named Cora. She wished to become a Christian, but was fearful of reprisals from "the women from the mesa." Cora had a young son whom she brought to the church with her, but sadly, he was dying from tuberculosis. "Oh, how pitiful he is yet how cheerful," Bertha related. Cora's husband, Andrew, was very angry with her for attending the church services. The missionaries asked that their friends pray for the souls of several who were unsaved, and living in sin: Earl Jackson, Fred Adams, Paul Takala, Ralph Carl, Robert Adams, and "Moody Lomesywea." According to the missionaries, there were two kinds of people, those who believed in God, and those who believed in Satan.

_◎))_

In June of 1936, Ethel wrote to Maud, thanking her for some gifts that she had sent. "And yes we got the things O.K. And we are very glad of it and thank you for it." In return, Ethel was sending some corn and a basket. She still made pottery, but she did not have any at that time. She did mention that her sister Hattie had been making some beautiful pottery, and even little Vivian was learning to work with the clay. Vivian had not made any pottery that summer because she was going to Miss Kirschke's summer school at the church. They had learned that the children who had perfect attendance would get prizes. Ethel wished that Maud could see Vivian. She could talk and sing— "she talk to much"—in Hopi, Tewa, and English.

Vivian was nearly four years old. Ethel was sending some pictures, and Maud would see that "she is a big girl." Ethel was still nursing Vivian, "she still like my milk." Of course, it was not uncommon that mothers at that time nursed their babies for several years. And given the uncertainty of crops and weather, it is very likely that there were times when a mother's milk was the only nourishment for a small child. It is no wonder that Ethel was proud that she could still nurse.

Ethel had recently made a dress from some fabric that Miss Ryan sent out to her. Ethel Ryan had never returned to First Mesa; she had permanently moved back to the East Coast, but they had resumed contact and sometimes wrote to each other. Ethel Muchvo had sent out some of her piiki, and in her letter to Maud, she explained how she made it: "This is the way I make piki. I put boiling water on the corn meils, and mix with it, and after that they put the cold water on it again and mix the ashes with water and put it in the dough to make it gray or blue."

Ethel wrote to Maud in November of that year, telling her that she had been very sick for over a month, but now she was feeling much better. "I never be felling well about one month, but now I am well now." Little Vivian had also had trouble. She had burned her feet when some boiling water spilled on her. That had been a month earlier, and, thankfully, now she was nearly completely recovered. Vivian had turned five years old the past August. It was getting cold out there, with winter coming, and Wilfred wanted to know if Maud would be able to send out an old coat for him. Ethel's letter was brief, just a page and a half, and her head was "ahcing" again, so she was just writing a few lines. She had never forgotten her friend, and she hoped that Maud had not forgotten her "tewa friend." She felt badly because she had not written for many months, but "I will be glad to here from you." Ethel also asked Maud to let her know if she had gotten the corn and a basket that she had sent earlier. "Good bye Mrs Melville Your friend Ethel Wilfred."

There is no correspondence from Ethel until late August of the following year, 1937, when Ethel wrote to Maud thanking her for the dresses that she had sent to Vivian for her sixth birthday that month. They fit her perfectly, and when she got them she had immediately put one on to wear. But Ethel was wondering why Maud had not written in such a long time, "Mrs Melville, I am think and think all the time, because you never write…and I am very sorry about it." Ethel thought that maybe Maud had forgotten about her. She asked her friend Ruth Takala if she had heard from the Melvilles because Ruth occasionally sold pottery and dolls to them, but Ruth had not heard from Maud either. Wilfred also had asked why Maud did not write anymore. Ethel had been at the church tying comforters and making quilts, and she told Miss Kirschke about it, too. But then they got the dresses for Vivian's birthday, and Ethel was very thankful for them.

The winter of 1936-37 had been a very hard one for the Hopis. There were severe storms and heavy snows, and the Hopis had suffered from a lot of illnesses. There had been many deaths during those cold months. Little Vivian had gotten very sick. Ethel wrote to Maud, "well Mrs Melville, we was havening a hard time out here. You don't [know] why, the little Vivian got very sick again, and we were so unhappy all the time. and you see her on the picture she was very fat, but now she is so thin." Vivian did recover, but Ethel did not make any pottery, and Wilfred did not make any dolls, "so our sugar and coffee are all gone." Fortunately, Ethel's sister Hattie had made some pottery that she was able to sell, and she gave the money to the Muchvos to get some food. And again, Ethel wrote, "Mrs Melville I am going to ask you for some old coldes for us, the coat shirts and pants, it was getting cold out here."

_◎))_

At the end of the following summer, Ethel wrote to Maud that there had been no rains, and they had no peaches, no corn or watermelons. The crops had failed, and Ethel was very worried about the coming fall and winter. "Every things dry out, we use to have lot of things to, but now we never eat some corn or waterleoms, so I am just think and think maybe we are not going get much corn this year." Ethel was grateful that Maud had sent the dresses to Vivian because she was using her small savings of cash to buy food, and nothing else.

She knew that without a good harvest, they would be having a lean and hungry time in the following months.

Wilfred had been staying on the mesa, participating in the Snake Dance. This ancient ceremony is a petition for rain; the participants are members of a warrior society. The Snake Dance is held in August when the summer rains are over, the springs have dried, and the scorching summer winds have shriveled the plants. Much of the ceremony is conducted in the underground kivas, and the more public part of the ritual is held in the plaza. The participants hold snakes in their mouths—including venomous rattlesnakes—while they dance in the plaza. Because of their resemblance to lightning, the snakes have an association with clouds and are the messengers to the spirits that bring life-giving rain. After the dance, the snakes are taken out of the village and are released in the Four Directions to return to their homes and call the clouds to bring rain to the land.

When Wilfred came down to the house, he saw the things that the Melvilles sent to Vivian and was also grateful that they had remembered her birthday. Now she had clothes to wear when she started school that fall. Since there were no crops to harvest, Wilfred went to Gallup, New Mexico, to trade and, hopefully, to get some money or food that would help the family through the coming months. Ethel asked Maud to tell Mr. Melville that she said goodbye to him. "Well goodby Mrs Melville, ansure my letter, I will be glad to here from you, your loving friend, Mrs Ethel Wilfred."

Three months later, on November 24, 1937, Ethel wrote her last letter to Maud. She had not written earlier because she had sore eyes, and she could not see. Ethel was in the early stages of trachoma, an eye infection that causes pain, swelling, and scarring. One Hopi related that it was described as feeling as though you had bits of sand in your eyes. Ultimately, the infection results in blindness. Ethel was losing her sight. "I haven't say thank you since when you sent then [the dresses for Vivian], you don't now why I did not write to you, because I have sore eye, that is why, but now I can see little better." Vivian was well and happy, and she loved school. But Wilfred was very, very ill, and could not get out of bed. It was getting cold, and Ethel asked if Carey had any old

*Vivian stands in front of her parents, displaying the same smile as her father. Wilfred has dressed for the occasion, donning his beautiful turquoise necklace. Ethel's face shows the strain of the years she spent nursing Wilfred and her unrelenting struggle to survive.*

underwear. Wilfred needed to stay warm, and Ethel thought that a pair of long johns would help. She also asked if they had an old cotton blanket. If they had those things, please "sent it out, we need then in a hurry, if you have then."

Ethel was supposed to be working and helping at the day school Vivian attended, but "I have no good eyes." She should also be sewing some winter clothes for Vivian, but she was just staying with Wilfred, taking care of him while he was ill. In a previous letter, Maud had asked how Ethel and Wilfred were getting along, but Ethel wrote that they had no sheep, they had no cows.

*Vivian is wearing a traditional Hopi dress, a black* manta *with a belt woven with geometric designs, and moccasins with white deerskin wrappings on her legs.*

Her sister Hattie had some sheep and cattle, and she was glad to hear that Maud had inquired about her. Hattie had a son, Ralph, who had recently married, "and he is merranig 3 mont ago, and his wife got a baby boy last weeks, and we give him Wilfred neam because he is his grandpapa." As aunt and uncle, traditionally referred to as parents or grandparents in the Hopi way, Ethel and Wilfred should have been there helping with the baby, weaving a blanket or making a quilt or helping to cook food for a naming ceremony. Wilfred should "carry the water up [to the mesa] for them but he is so sick, he is in bed, and I am just staing with Wilfred and did not make any things for his baby."

Ethel never wrote to Maud again. She was going blind, and Wilfred was in the last stages of tuberculosis. Life became very sad and hard for Ethel. Without Wilfred to herd sheep and plant corn, the family had little food. And, without her eyes, Ethel could not make pottery to sell or trade. She closed her last letter, "Mrs Melville please sent this old things that I ask for it if you have then we need then in a hurry. from your loving friend Ethel Wilfred."

_◎)_

In the spring of 1938, Bertha Kirschke also wrote a last letter to the Melvilles. They had never met, but since Ethel Ryan had left Hopi country a few years earlier, Bertha continued to write to Maud now and then, giving her news of the people at First Mesa. She also mailed packages of film containing photos she had taken for the Melvilles, or film shot by Ethel and Wilfred using the camera that the Melvilles had given to them. But, just as Abigail Johnson and Ethel Ryan had been forced to take time off from their missionary efforts because the stress and burdens of work were causing serious health problems, so was Bertha Kirschke leaving First Mesa and returning to her home in Canada in an effort to regain some strength and health.

With the departure of Bertha Kirschke, even though there was a constant missionary presence on First Mesa, many of the people who had sporadically attended Christian services at the First Mesa Baptist Church returned to their traditional Hopi religion. Sewing days and quilting bees at the church were still popular, as were the Christmas celebrations with the feast and the gifts of toys and quilts and clothing. But the number of converts remained very low. In her last letter to Maud, Bertha wrote that she had cashed Maud's check and had given four dollars to Ethel Muchvo, and had kept one dollar for herself for postage. She did not mention if this money was a gift to help Ethel and her family, or if it was for the sale of some pottery. She did comment that she had not seen Ethel much that year. Ethel had been very busy, very involved with the dances and ceremonies up on the mesa.

_◎))_

Ethel did return to her traditional Hopi life and religion, and she always took part in ceremonies, including the woman's Basket Dance. And little Vivian, the last of her twelve children, never did contract her father's dreaded tuberculosis. She grew up to be a beautiful, petite, and active woman who married and eventually became a grandmother. Ethel taught her daughter to get up early every day and pray to the sun. Together they would walk up the trail to the mesa to visit friends and family. Ethel remained devoted to Wilfred. Although Hopi women can easily "divorce" a husband by simply asking him to leave her house and by putting his belongings outside of the door, telling him to go back to his mother's house, Ethel believed that a woman should be loyal to her husband, and should stay with just one man. She nursed Wilfred through years of illness, and when the burden of providing for her family fell on her shoulders, she worked to make her pottery to sell to buy food for her family when Wilfred was too sick to herd a flock of sheep or to plant corn. Even when Wilfred sold his flock of sheep to buy the clothing and other things he would need to return to a traditional life, to dance in a kachina ceremony—even though his actions in the short term created hardships for the family—Ethel stayed true to Wilfred.

Every spring Ethel planted a large garden next to her house, raising a plot of corn and melons. She also tended a large orchard of fruit trees and grape plants. In spite of her poverty, and having a husband who often was bedridden, Ethel was a remarkable and strong woman who remained optimistic and practical, doing all that she could to provide for her family. Her relationship with Maud was one of friendship, but also one of business and practicality. Ethel sent many wonderful gifts of pottery, kachinas, Wilfred's hand-woven belts, piiki, and dried corn to Maud. And Maud valued and treasured her Hopi arts and Ethel's gifts.

There was also a years-long exchange of photographs and family news between the Muchvos and the Melvilles. Ethel wrote to the Melville children when they went away to school, and she sent gifts when they married. However, on the practical side, Ethel also counted on Maud's gifts of used coats for Wilfred, dresses for Vivian and herself, a blanket, a saw for making kachinas, and lengths of fabric to sew into clothing. Each fall as the days grew shorter and the summer heat faded, Ethel's letters often began, "it is getting cold out here." And even though the clothes and shoes and blankets were secondhand, used items, through the Depression years they were still very valued gifts, and nearly impossible to obtain out on the mesas. With her circle of friends in Worcester, Maud could more easily get these used clothes to send to Ethel. Maud's boxes of clothes and shoes saw the Muchvos through many hard winters out at First Mesa, where the trails were rocky and muddy, there was no electricity or plumbing, water and firewood were mostly hauled by hand, and homes were heated with wood. Through her membership in many clubs, and her Hopi talks, Maud was able to sell Ethel's pottery and Wilfred's kachinas, most importantly at times when the local traders were not buying. There were also times when Maud sent money to purchase some of the more expensive items, such as the drum and the belt and the turquoise necklace. Maud's gifts, her purchases, and her warm letters were often life-sustaining for Ethel, as well as for her family.

Wilfred succumbed to tuberculosis in early June 1942. Making pottery was more difficult for Ethel as she lost her sight. Vivian recalled that when her mother "got blind," losing her eyesight was one of the hardest trials of her life, and often, they would cry together. The light of summer—the happy family years with her husband and daughter, and her productive years as a potter—had faded into the fall of her life. But Ethel carried on, living nearly thirty more years. Sellie, another potter who lived nearby, proved to be a true friend in need. Every morning Sellie would walk to Coyote Springs to get two heavy buckets of water—one for her, and the other for Ethel. Ethel, meanwhile, would cook the morning meal for the three of them. After Vivian left for school each day, the two women spent many companionable hours doing their work together, until Sellie went back down the hill to her house in the afternoon.

Vivian recalled one memorable time when Ethel was staying up on the mesa, and she became very sick, nearly dying. Through that illness, she saw angels who were the spirits of her dead children. They flew to her to give her something to eat. But she did not take it. In the Hopi way, if you eat such food, you would die. Sometimes during a critical illness, the spirit can take a journey when a person is on the border between life and death. Sometimes dreams represent this temporary departure of the spirit from the body. In the Hopi belief, the spirit exists even in the absence of the body; this is not unlike the idea that when a man dies, he merely wakes up. Ethel refused the food from those spirits, and she lived. She wanted to stay on the earth to be with her daughter Vivian. Ethel had returned to the traditional Hopi life with its year-round ceremonial calendar, and the ancient wisdom of the people sustained her through her illnesses, blindness, and other hard times.

Ethel taught Vivian to make pottery, and for many years after she was an adult, Vivian saved some pieces of her mother's unfired pots. But they were stored on a ledge up by the roof in Vivian's home in Hano, and during one huge thunderstorm, the roof leaked, and all of Ethel's pots, the last pots that she had made, turned to mud. Vivian always felt very sad about losing those last pieces of her mother's work. Since Ethel always had to sell her pottery, Vivian has no surviving pieces of her mother's bowls and vases.

After the late 1930s, Ethel and Maud apparently stopped writing to each other—or perhaps they did continue to correspond, but unfortunately, no later letters exist. Very likely, the circumstances of their lives changed. Wilfred became very ill and died in 1942, and Ethel was having more trouble with her eyes. It became impossible for her to write a letter. Maud's children married and had children of their own. As Maud's family grew larger and she became a grandmother, she would have had different interests and responsibilities.

*Maud and Carey Melville later in life.*

Additionally, the years of World War II changed the lives and the focus of everyone in the country for most of the 1940s.

Maud and her husband did make one last trip to First Mesa in about 1953. She was seventy-three, and Carey was seventy-five. Ethel would have been in her late seventies, and by that time, she had gone blind. Certainly a trip to Arizona would have been a strenuous undertaking for people of the Melvilles' ages. The traveling time alone would have been longer and more complicated than it is now. They could have taken a train west, but then would have had to arrange transportation from Holbrook or Winslow up to First Mesa. At that time most of the roads to the mesas were still just dirt tracks. And, just as it had been in the 1920s, at the time of their first visit, tourists on the mesas were still fairly rare, so there were no hotels or restaurants to accommodate visitors.

But something about the Hopi people, the mesas and pueblo homes, and the beautiful Hopi pottery and other arts had taken hold in Maud's heart. She was enchanted with the music, the haunting, chanting melodies, the ancient kachina songs. For all of her life, she had a deep love and connection to the Hopi people, even though she probably only had superficial knowledge of their traditions, their history, and their deeply religious lifestyle. Perhaps part of the attraction was the harsh and dramatic landscape of the Hopi country, with its craggy, desert-tan sandstone cliffs, the immense skies, and the purple shadows of the canyons and the sunsets. There is a sense of ancient timelessness in the Hopi landscape, and it could not have been more opposite from the lush, green Eastern landscape of Maud's home. The arid country of the Southwest does not hold that appeal for everyone who experiences it, but to Maud, it was a lifelong attraction.

There was also the personal connection, the friendship between Ethel and Maud, the two women who had corresponded for a decade. They were mothers and wives together, they had experienced illness and loss, they had gained the wisdom that comes through years of living. They also had a connection, a kinship that only comes through the years, the decades of association, of sharing family stories, the woes and laughter. They shared an everlasting friendship formed during that long ago Hopi summer.

During that last visit in the winter of their lives, Maud and Ethel would have known that it would be the last time they would see each other. Regretfully, there are no letters or photographs that can give a glimpse into the hours they spent together, the meals, the walks, the reminiscing. Maud would have met Vivian, the light and joy of Ethel's life. She would very likely have visited with Ethel's sister Hattie, and her friend Sellie. Perhaps Maud brought photographs of her family, but Ethel could not see them. Probably the two old ladies, one a New England matron, the other a blind Hopi potter, sat outside and felt the Arizona sun on their faces or the cool shade by the side of Ethel's stone house. Perhaps they sang the Hopi songs together.

*Ethel Muchvo, 1965. Photo by Byron Hunter.*

Polacca Arizarea,
Nov. 2 4 1937.

Dear Mrs. Melville.
I thank very much for the dresses that you sent for, Vivian. I havent say thank you since when you sent then, you dont now why I did not write, to you, because I have sore, eye, that is why, but now I can see lettle better. and Vivian is very well, she like to go to, school. and her father Wilfred, is not well he is sick. he is, Quick sick. and I was wundering if Mr Melville has amany old, under ware, and allso the old cotton blanck to sent it out.

_◎))_

Ethel died on February 22, 1970. Vivian said that her mother was very old—
she believed that she was in her nineties—but since she never had a birth cer-
tificate, she was not sure how many years her mother had lived. Ethel's sister,
Hattie Carl, also died in 1970. She was older than Ethel, and through recalling

dates and years and various events, her family calculated that Hattie was 104 years old when she passed away. Maud also survived into her nineties. Carey passed away in 1963, at the age of eighty-five. Maud remained very active and involved in her community until 1971 when she fell and broke her hip. She died six years later, in 1977, at ninety-seven.

Maud believed that Hopi music and song was a window into the Hopi soul and spirit, that music was the communicating link between the Hopis and their gods. She studied the music and collected songs. In every one of Maud's lectures, she included a quote from Natalie Curtis's 1923 book on Pueblo Indian art and music:

*The wind sweeping the crags and whirling down the trail has carved its strange melody on the Indian's mind even as it has carved on the rocks in the curious erosion the record of its presence. Its echo is heard in the song of the Hopi through desert solitudes. There in that wide land under the blaze of the Arizona sun, amid the shifting color of the tinted sands and the purple blue of the shadows must the songs be heard to be heard truly.*

Ethel knew the songs—they were the songs from her home, the songs from her heart. Maud heard the songs.

*Maud Melville hiking up the steep trail out of the Grand Canyon.*

# BIBLIOGRAPHY

Billingsley, M. W. *Behind the Scenes in Hopi Land.* Privately printed, 1974.

Breunig, Robert, and Michael Lomatuway'ma. "Hopi Kachina Dolls." *Plateau Journal,* Volume 63, Number 4, 1992.

———. "Hopi Scenes of Everyday Life." *Plateau Journal,* Volume 55, Number 1, 1983.

Colton, Harold S. *Hopi Kachina Dolls with a Key to their Identification.* Albuquerque, New Mexico: University of New Mexico Press, 1959.

Curtis, Natalie. *The Indians' Book: Authentic Native American Legends, Lore & Music.* New York: Bonanza Books, 1987.

Finger, Judith W., and Andrew D. Finger. *Circles of Life: Katsina Imagery on Hopi Wicker Basketry.* Ukiah, California: Grace Hudson Museum and Sun House, 2006.

James, Harry C. *Pages from Hopi History.* Tucson, Arizona: University of Arizona Press, 1974.

Johnson, Abigail E. *Beyond the Black Buttes: True Stories of Hopiland.* Kansas City, Missouri: Western Baptist Publishing Company, 1934.

Means, Florence Crannell. *The Rains Will Come.* Cambridge, Massachusetts: Riverside Press, 1954.

———. *Sunlight on the Hopi Mesas.* Philadelphia, Pennsylvania: Judson Press, 1960.

O'Kane, Walter Collins. *The Hopis: Portrait of a Desert People.* Norman, Oklahoma: University of Oklahoma Press, 1969.

Page, Susanne, and Jake Page. *Hopi.* New York: Harry N. Abrams Publishers, 1994.

Schaaf, Gregory. *American Indian Baskets I.* Santa Fe, New Mexico: CIAC Press, 2006.

Silas, Anna. *Journey to Hopi Land.* Tucson, Arizona: Rio Nuevo Publishers, 2006.

Teiwes, Helga. *Hopi Basket Weaving: Artistry in Natural Fibers.* Tucson, Arizona: University of Arizona Press, 1996.

Walker, Willard, and Lydia L. Wykoff. *Hopis, Tewas, and the American Road.*
Albuquerque, New Mexico: University of New Mexico Press, 1986.

## ADDITIONAL SUGGESTED READING

Blair, Mary Ellen, and Laurence Blair. *The Legacy of a Master Potter: Nampeyo and Her Descendants.* Tucson, Arizona: Rio Nuevo Publishers, 1999.

Day, Jonathan. *Traditional Hopi Kachinas: A New Generation of Carvers.* Flagstaff, Arizona: Northland Publishing, 2000.

Kavena, Juanita Tiger. *Hopi Cookery.* Tucson, Arizona: University of Arizona Press, 1981.

Kosik, Fran. *Native Roads: The Complete Motoring Guide to the Navajo and Hopi Nations,* 2nd ed. Tucson, Arizona: Rio Nuevo Publishers, 2005.

McManis, Kent. *A Guide to Hopi Katsina Dolls.* Tucson, Arizona: Rio Nuevo Publishers, 2000.

Messier, Kim, and Pat Messier. *Hopi & Pueblo Tiles: An Illustrated History.* Tucson, Arizona: Rio Nuevo Publishers, 2007.

Udall, Louise. *Me and Mine: The Life Story of Helen Sekaquaptewa.* Tucson, Arizona: University of Arizona Press, 1969.

# ACKNOWLEDGMENTS

MANY PEOPLE GAVE TIME AND ADVICE in helping to research the letters and photographs for this volume. Nothing, however, could have happened without the generous help of Robert Arnold, who shared his grandfather's photographs, his grandmother's trip journal, and the many letters she so carefully saved from her Hopi friends, Ethel Salyah Muchvo and Ruth Takala, and the missionaries at First Mesa.

Wesleyan University has, likewise, made Maud Melville's letters and notes and Indian arts collection available for research and study. Juliana Shortell, the collections manager in the anthropology department, has answered many, many questions and e-mails. She took time from her busy schedule to provide copies of all the Melville photos and papers, and she provided information about identifying signatures and marks on the Hopi pottery and other art objects. Juliana's help has gone beyond the requirements of her work, and I am grateful for her assistance.

And of course, I could not have begun to do this work without the help and support of so many Hopi people. I truly was not prepared for the generous sharing of information and stories. Many of the Hopis freely contributed their knowledge of families and genealogy, introduced me to friends who could help, invited me into their homes, shared photographs, and showed me treasured pieces of family memorabilia. It was not uncommon for each Hopi person I met to spend hours going through every photograph in the Melville collection. The detailed information they shared went beyond anything that I had hoped for; and even though some of the material they gave me is not relevant to this story, that material is now archived with the Hopi Tribe for the future use of scholars and the Hopi people.

I had also not anticipated just how much fun this work would be. I already knew many Hopis, but I met so many more marvelous people. I was royally fed at nearly every house, because sharing food is a core attribute of the Hopis, and I was often given gifts of food and bread and corn, kachinas and rattles. And it was not uncommon for a Hopi with whom I was talking to jump up and say, "Let's go," and we would be off to see Polacca Wash or Ispa Spring or to visit a cousin or neighbor.

On one grand adventure, Lynette Shupla offered to take me to Coyote Springs to see the field house where her grandmother, Nellie, wove her gigantic basket. Unfortunately, because of previous commitments, we could not leave until late afternoon. Rains threatened as we left Shungopavi, and the skies darkened as we traveled south. The summer monsoon rains turned the roads into a deep and slippery mud soup. We slipped and slid along the road, using the lowest of the 4 x 4 gears, and sometimes drove across the desert to avoid particularly deep and water-covered arroyos.

Our little one-hour jaunt turned into an hours-long ordeal—and adventure—as we tried to make our way through the darkness, back to the highway, traveling on a maze of mud tracks. As the sun dropped and dark shadows covered the hills, the rains began, and the car's windshield wipers pushed more mud than rain off the windows. After anxious hours of slipping and spinning over the muddy tracks, we eventually found our way back to the highway and to Second Mesa, and we fervently agreed that on the next attempt to find Nellie's sheep camp, we would leave earlier in the day, and after the rainy season.

Ethel Muchvo's daughter, Vivian, spent many hours looking at the Hopi photographs. Vivian took me to Polacca to show me her mother's house, the orchard and the fields where she planted corn, and the place at the edge of the

*Young Maud, Robert, Martha, and Maud on the trail to the bottom of the Grand Canyon.*

hill where Ethel had fired her beautiful pottery. While we talked about the pictures, Vivian's delightful granddaughters listened attentively to her stories of growing up at the base of First Mesa, making pottery with her mother.

Edison and Karen Tootsie spent many hours helping to find the families of the people in the old black-and-white photographs. Edison's sister, Virgina Benally, gave me information on the early years of the First Mesa Baptist Church. Emory Sekaquaptewa gave me suggestions and corrections to factual information, and Hartman Lomawaima also helped to identify buildings and villages in the photographs. Jennie Holtsoi, her daughter, Margaret, and son-in-law, John Williams, shared stories about Hattie Carl, Ethel Muchvo's sister. June Clown and Elsie Tumes gave me information about their great-grand-mother, Sellie.

William T. Beaver spent several hours going over the photographs and sharing information on names and places. He also read the manuscript and contributed much valuable information based on his many years of living and working on the Hopi and Navajo Reservations. Other people who helped were Marlene Sekaquaptewa, Lynette Shupla, Lloyd and Lydia Mansfield, Martha Looyahoema, Loretta Yestewa, Fletcher Healing, Rick Koruh, Rosalita Lalo, John Lomavaya, Willis Lomavaya, and Bruce Augah. Leigh Kuwanwisiwma, director, and Stewart Koyiyumptewa, archivist, of the Hopi Cultural Preservation Office, gave their support to the project and suggested some people to contact for more information. To all of them, and to the many more people who showed support and gave suggestions for learning more about the photographs, I wish to give my most heartfelt thanks. This book could not have been written without the support and good wishes of the Hopi people. I hope that the photographs and stories will bring enjoyment to all who see them. Overall, my intent was to honor the people who showed such strength and wisdom in those hard years, the years of the Hopi summer. And privately, I will feel proud if this effort makes a small contribution to sharing and preserving the amazing history of the Hopi people.